LOVE, LIFE,

AND THE SHADOW

OF DEATH

AN UNFORGETTABLE JOURNEY

KIM DOKE FLETTER

Love, Life, and the Shadow of Death
An Unforgettable Journey
by Kim Doke Fletter

Printed in the United States of America

ISBN 9781498402255

www.xulonpress.com

Table of Contents

Chapter 1: A New Life and Adventure......................11
Chapter 2: The Day of Bad News..........................27
Chapter 3: Carrots, Carrots, and More Carrots! 33
Chapter 4: Pressing On for an Answer.....................36
Chapter 5: In the Hands of a Doctor......................44
Chapter 6: Life Goes On...56
Chapter 7: The Medical Trek..................................61
Chapter 8: Houston, Here We Come! 66
Chapter 9: Land of the Unknowns...........................71
Chapter 10: Cabin Life—A New Adventure 91
Chapter 11: A Perilous March, but to Victory?........109
Chapter 12: Pressing Towards the Goal..................132
Chapter 13: The Tumor Is Winning! 153
Chapter 14: God's Call to Minister 161
Chapter 15: Uncharted Days.................................165
Chapter 16: Forever My Hero 168
Chapter 17: The Move Next Door...........................175
Chapter 18: The Kingdom Nears 178
Chapter 19: Hospital Is Home 184
Chapter 20: The Kingdom Cometh! 190
Chapter 21: Remembrances...................................199
Chapter 22: Words of Wisdom...............................208

Dedication

To the memory of Robert "Bob" Doke
You are my hero.
I will always love you!

Acknowledgments

I thank and praise my Lord and Savior, for without Him, this story would not be told.

Thank you to those who prayed for us during Bob's fight. Your prayers were heard in heaven!

Thank you, Dorothy "Del" Kinsey (Bob's mom), for all your research when Bob was diagnosed and for your proofreading and faithful prayers during the process of writing.

I thank my niece, Rachel Edge Collins, for her labor of love in editing.

Thank you to everyone who colored the threads that wove the beautiful tapestry of our lives to be able to tell our story. I love you!

And I thank music artists Mark Schultz and Andrew Peterson for their beautiful songs that ministered deep within my soul as I walked through what felt like the valley of the shadow of death—Mark Schultz: "He Will Carry Me" and Andrew Peterson: "Alaska or Bust," "Nothing to Say," "High Noon," "After the Last Tear Falls," "Faith to Be Strong," "The Queen of Iowa," "More," and "Let Me Sing"

Not to us, O Lord, not to us,
but to Your name give glory
Because of Your lovingkindness, because of Your truth.
—Psalm 115:1, NASB

CHAPTER 1

A New Life and Adventure

"Life is good!" Isn't that a screen print on a T-shirt? Well, sometimes life is good, but sometimes it's better than good. After all, when you're in great health, live in a beautiful place, and have a wonderful marriage, a thriving business, rental income, and a husband with a personality that draws out the best in anyone, could you ask for anything more? And that's just the beginning of how good life was, living in the north Georgia mountains with Bob.

God's glorious creation is all around here in the north Georgia mountains, abounding with purple mountain-silhouetted sunrises and sunsets; lush, dew-covered valleys; and vibrant streams, rivers, and waterfalls teeming with life, excitement, and inexpressible beauty as they make their way from the mountains down to the sea and back again.

Bob and I moved to Cleveland, Georgia, from Fort Lauderdale, Florida, in November 1989 after growing up in Florida and pursuing worthwhile, lucrative careers. As children growing up in the late sixties and seventies in Fort Lauderdale, we experienced the beauty, innocence, and joy of a simpler time. We met in August 1974 and fell in love after only a two-week courtship. I was eighteen, and he was twenty-one. Bob quickly proposed, sending his family into temporary shock, as he had previously stated he was a happy bachelor with no marital interests, and we married in November of that same year.

The city of Fort Lauderdale is known as the "Venice of America" because of its intricate and beautiful waterways that mingle with the deep-blue Atlantic Ocean. It is truly a tropical paradise. Fort Lauderdale also became a haven for beachgoers after the famous 1960s movie *Where the Boys Are* was filmed there. It became a mecca for college students on spring break.

The area's cultural landscape continued to evolve, and Bob and I knew we wanted to experience something different. Even though we lived in an affluent neighborhood, we witnessed our neighbors running down the middle of the street screaming at each other over drugs. We longed for the days of our youth when you knew your neighbors, they knew you, and you both had each other's interests at heart. We thus searched for a place that we thought had all the components of a simpler life: a small piece of land, a rural neighborhood with caring neighbors, and a place where your word and a handshake still meant something.

When we began our search, we considered northern Georgia, eastern Tennessee, and the Carolinas, where we could experience a different culture, seasons, and a little snow. I say "a little snow" because we were native Floridians and didn't know how we would be able to handle the winter months in another region. We also didn't want to be more than a day's drive away from our families. We had visited the eastern United States mountain region many times and loved the tristate area.

The more we talked about moving, the more we knew it was something we wanted to do. We made a budget and determined how much money we could actually survive on. Next, we researched what kinds of jobs we could obtain and decided on the minimum salary we would need after downsizing. After gathering real estate books, we went to work planning our new future.

We planned a vacation and traveled all around the tri-state area, finally settling on the little town of Cleveland, Georgia. A high school friend of Bob's had moved there, and when he found out we were interested in moving north, he invited us to come for a visit and check the area out. He raved about how much he liked it there and encouraged us to come and stay with him for the week. He had a beautiful home on Lake Lanier, and since we hadn't seen him in a long time, we eagerly accepted.

After seeing the availability of employment and housing in the surrounding area, we quickly realized that this would be our new home. Jobs were plentiful, and new houses were springing up in the countryside. There was a house that caught our eye, and we didn't hesitate to put down earnest money to purchase it. The house had one and a quarter acres and allowed horses. The covenants stated you could have one horse per acre, and Bob used to tease, "Oh, we can have one horse and a quarter horse."

We drove back to Fort Lauderdale, gave a month's notice at work, began packing, and moved that November. Our friends thought we were absolutely crazy! They felt the same as we did, wanting a simpler life, but were too afraid to take the plunge and lose their good salaries. We knew life was too precious to not be valued and enjoyed, so we set out on a quest to pursue our dreams.

Not long after moving into our newly purchased small country homestead, we began to familiarize ourselves with the north Georgia lifestyle. We often took afternoon breaks from unpacking and explored the countryside, intrepidly venturing down forest service roads in our newly acquired Ford Bronco. This sometimes included fording creeks, which was concerning at times because of the swift water that flowed under our vehicle. Our pioneering became a jovial tease with our native-born neighbors, as they would often say, "You know more roads, shortcuts, and points of interest than we do, and we've lived here all our lives."

The population of Cleveland was just around twelve thousand at the time, and life there was good, innocent, fun, fresh, and exciting. We were not accustomed to seeing lush green countryside; wildflowers blanketing the roadside; hills dotted with cows, deer, and wild turkeys; layers of blue-hued mountains at every turn; creeks, streams, and waterfalls; and neighbors that greeted you with hot homemade biscuits and jelly.

After spending a month getting settled and exploring the area, we knew it was time to start searching for jobs. We dreaded it because that month had been one of the best times of our lives, yet we knew we needed to get back to work. Bob started searching first and found a construction job. Then he found a more permanent position in maintenance with a bank that had the benefits we desired. After working there a few years, he was asked to become an apprentice for a local locksmith shop that he had frequented on bank business. He quickly accepted, since he saw it as a great opportunity to learn more about the trade. The owner was willing to give on-the-job training, and Bob was mechanically inclined, so he didn't think twice. It also paid more than what he was making at the bank.

My experience in Fort Lauderdale had been managing a data-entry department several years for a Fortune 500 company. Since I had data-entry experience, I worked at an international mail-order company, taking phone orders. Our former careers were one factor that prompted our move. Bob and I realized that our careers had come to own us. Our jobs were extremely stressful, and we needed jobs that didn't demand that kind of sacrificial dedication anymore. The stress and long hours of our jobs had become consuming to the degree that we felt life was literally passing us by. We were keeping up with the Joneses simply because we had successful careers—buying that home with the manicured lawn and pool.

When you work under a production schedule, you quickly realize it will either make you or break you. And if you make it, you perform autonomously in order to survive. I knew I couldn't continue in that mode for another decade without seeing destructive results in my personal life, so Bob and I determined that our careers would never again own us. We were certainly thankful for the opportunities those jobs granted us, but we knew we wanted more out of life—not what the world considers as more, but more of what we had experienced as youths, living a less hectic and less materialistic life, taking time to care for others. We would be faithful and dedicated employees, but that was it!

Bob, after working for the locksmith a few years, decided that the north Georgia area needed a locksmith service. He approached his boss with the idea of having a satellite office that he could run, but it fell on deaf ears. After much careful thought and calculation, he decided to start his own business in Cleveland, Georgia, in 1993 with another friend who was a locksmith. I continued to work full-time at the international mail-order company and rode with him on service calls when I was off.

Initially, to gain all the business he could, he became a AAA service contractor and signed with other car clubs as well. In the locksmith business, Bob was on call 24/7, and he never knew where he might end up during the course of a day. From helping a person who had lost their keys hiking the Appalachian Trail, to a frightened mother in the grocery-store parking lot who had locked her keys in her car with a crying child inside, we knew from the very beginning that this trade was going to be a roller coaster of new adventures.

One memorable experience occurred when we were dispatched on a call that came in around 11 p.m. from AAA Auto Club. Since it was deep in the national forest in Franklin, North Carolina, we knew it was going to be a late night when we considered the turnaround time. After arriving in the general vicinity of the designated area, we began to ascend a forest service road, searching for our customer. Since a forest service road is usually used only by the forest park rangers, it can be very primitive if it is not maintained or frequently traveled. Some roads had huge potholes, boulders from a landslide, sections washed out from heavy rains, or even wild brush that invaded the roadbed.

As we continued to ascend, I realized we were beginning to lose our cell-phone service, so I immediately called Bob's mom to tell her our location, just to be on the side of caution. As we continued our trek up this dark and winding road for several miles and still did not locate our customer, I began to become anxious, saying, "Bob, maybe we should turn around. We should have found them by now!"

Bob was always tenacious about helping his customers until the job was completed. And if it meant driving down dirt roads that would only be in an Indiana Jones movie, well, let the adventure begin! Some roads were so steep I would hang onto my seat, wondering if our fully loaded service van would make it; or the roads were so virgin at times that brush and trees scraped both sides of our vehicle, leaving us with dents to prove our backwoods rendezvous. The keys would rattle so much that you thought they were going to fall off their hooks. Bob considered most roads passable and didn't think twice about fording a flowing stream, all in the name of persistence to service his stranded customer.

Now approximately ten miles into the national forest, I was getting very nervous and began to plead with Bob to turn around. It was pitch-black, and we continued to ascend on the mountain ridge. He amazed me once again with his incredible dedication as he said, "No, Kim, we are continuing on. They've got to be here somewhere; they made the call." We were truly in the middle of nowhere. I mean nowhere! We were so deep in the national forest that if anything happened to us, I was sure we would not be found for days. It was so black that the stars were center stage and their brilliance illuminated against the jet-black sky. It was as if they were beckoning, "Look at me, my magnificence, God's creation!"

We continued to ascend all the more, still with no cell-phone connection. As Bob forged on another mile, lo and behold, around the next bend there was a tiny campfire visible deep in a hollow. After we manuevered a long descent to arrive at this campsite, a small group of men emerged and began to clap. They were elated and amazed to see us. It was like a breath of fresh air for me too! I gasped in relief, especially when I saw that they were just a group of businessmen. I said, "Praise God! They *are* here! We finally found them!" I'm sure Bob breathed a sigh of relief too, to have his very anxious wife stop pleading to abandon the call. You can only imagine that I had thoughts of coming upon a group of wild motorcycle riders who had nothing but bad intentions. I chuckle now at how the story ended.

The one who had locked his keys in his car was a salesman, and because of his extreme gratitude for Bob's perseverance, he gave us several samples of his products that he had on hand: pancake mix; mini bottles of syrup, coffee, pretzels; and bags of various kinds of chips. We discovered that they were just on a weekend getaway. What a surprise for me! And I can't tell you how delighted I was to be wrapping up that call and heading out of that national forest and back into civilization.

Even though I don't care to relive that night's adventure, I do believe that everyone should experience being deep in the forest at least once in his or her lifetime. You can hear the sounds of God's creation and see the stars in our galaxy like you've never seen them before. And, if you listen close enough, you can even hear and sense nature in her resting state of glory. "The heavens are telling of the glory of God; and their expanse is declaring the work of His hands" (Psalm 19:1, NASB).

Bob never complained about his occupation, even though it meant that he could be summoned twenty-four hours a day. He was the owner and his own boss, so he was in control of his work schedule. He actually put on his business card, just for a joke, "Open 7 Days a Week—23-Hour Emergency Service." When his customers inquired, "Why twenty-three hours?" he loved to explain that the missing hour was for his wife, and then he would laugh. No matter how many times they asked, he was always delighted to explain with his witty response. We traveled together as much as we could, never knowing if we were going to have dinner in some remote town or would be blazing a new trail, adding to our already long list of adventuresome discoveries.

One night in the summer months, which was one of our busiest seasons, we were on our way home around 1 a.m. and received a call from a customer in distress at a local campground. That entire day we had bounced back and forth between three counties on numerous service calls for AAA Auto Club and were getting weary, ready to go home. After completing the last call at 1:30 a.m. in a campground on Lake Burton, Bob drove to a distant part of the campground to reveal a beautiful lake, anticipating the moment since the night was clear and the moonlight bright. He had been on service calls to this campground before, and on this night he kept it a secret as he drove, revealing this surprise to me for the first time. The view was of a private inlet of the lake. We stopped, got out, and stood on the shore for a moment, feeling a cool breeze on our faces. Holding each other tightly, we watched the moonlight as it danced on each ripple of the water. No words were necessary. We immersed ourselves in the stillness and glory of the moment, taking it all in.

There was not a thing Bob missed in enjoying the beauty of God's creation. While traveling the country roads, he would often notice the shape and silhouette of a tree without its leaves contrasted against the bright-blue sky, the pattern and shape of a windblown cloud or leaf as it drifted through the air, the sun's glistening reflection on an icy snow-covered tree limb, or a wildflower that had bloomed in its own special place on the side of the road.

One fall day while we were riding through the mountains, a fanfare of leaves swirled through the air as the wind fashioned their path. They surged right toward our windshield, causing feelings of exhilaration and excitement. From then on, whenever we saw the leaves dance in a free fall on a windy day, we called it a "leaf shower." We always noticed the things in life that most people take for granted or even sometimes consider a nuisance.

On one occasion, we went to Saluda, North Carolina, for a weekend getaway. My brother's daughter, Anna, who was three, squatted down to discover a newfound leaf that was tossing about over a metal grate. Bob noticed what she was doing, bent over, and watched with her as the leaf fluttered. It fluttered because as it lay over the grate, winds intermittently rushed up beneath it, causing it to skip about. Bob got down on his knees and played with the leaf, making it flutter more. It so excited little Anna that Bob would take time to go into her little world. She loved her Uncle Bob and was drawn to him like a magnet.

In Bob's business, since we never knew what town or county we would end up in, I had to learn to adopt the mind-set of going with the flow. Bob and I could have allowed the necessity of remaining mobile to make us miserable, as it certainly changed our lifestyle, but we both had decided that life is what you make it. You can choose to be miserable at your job when it goes against your wishes, or you can adapt and try to look for the blessings in it.

At first, I let the demand of being on call get to me. I used to love to have people over for dinner, and after several business-related interruptions, I realized having guests for dinner was not going to fit into our new life-style. Customers were going to call, and they would have to come first. They were our business, and expanding it was our priority. I could either fight it, which would have caused Bob and me to eventually grow apart, or I could join him. After all, I had encouraged him when his company was being conceived, and now that it was birthed and growing, I needed to be his ally.

One day when he received a long-distance call, I decided to stay home to do some things. After he left, I began to have a pity party, wishing he had a nine-to-five job instead. The Lord quickly reminded me of how I had encouraged him to start his business and that I needed to stop complaining and join him in his efforts and business venture. I thought about how doctors, nurses, EMTs, firefighters, and other professionals sacrifice their entire lives, time, and families to pursue their careers, and it humbled me. Just as I had once needed their service for a medical emergency, I knew that Bob was also providing a service. He often softened the frustration or fear that a customer was feeling in his time of need. From then on, I tried to be as flexible and mobile as I could, riding with him on service calls and taking something with me that I could work on. Since I taught a Sunday school class, I would often take lessons to study, cards or notes to write, books to read, or even bills to pay.

Bob and I loved antiques, and when a call brought us to an area with antique stores, we would stop and shop until the next call came in, sending us in a new direction. We always looked for rustic items or hunt-ing-and-fishing decor to decorate our rental cabins. Bob would often come across some mounted deer head, fox, or flying goose that had seen better days, allowing us to get it for a great price. He would excitedly call me over to get my opinion, although he had already made up his mind, saying, "Honey, what do you think of this? Wouldn't it be great in the cabin?" I remember I would have that look of, *Oh no, what did you find now?* on my face as I strolled toward him to see his discovery. Even after my disenchanted response, Bob would eagerly pur-chase his newfound treasure. I must admit, somehow they always proved useful, bringing the look and feel of the great outdoors to just the right spot inside our cabins.

Another display of Bob's happy-go-lucky attitude and love for his business was when he got a call around 3 a.m. to service someone who was over an hour away. Two couples had arrived at their cabin in the mountains, saying, "We've left our keys at home in Atlanta and don't want to have to drive back to get them. Can you make us a key?" Without hesitation, Bob said yes. That meant he would have to pick the lock open and then make a key. He hurriedly jumped out of bed, put on his clothes, and sprinted out the door while dancing a little jig, saying, "I get to go to work—someone's waiting to pay me!"

In my grogginess, I rose up to say, "Man, are you crazy? I thought, *It's the middle of the night, you're leaving your warm bed, and yet you are dancing a jig to go to work.*

In selfishness, I must admit, there were times when I asked Bob to turn a call down because it meant I would be worrying until he returned home. I worried because of the steep mountainous roads he so often had to cross, and depending on the season, they sometimes were so covered in fog you could hardly see in front of your vehicle. One time we had to open the door to use the side of the road as a guide. Other times there were storms with tornado warnings or blinding rain on the downside of the mountain. But Bob's attitude, pressing forward as if there was an inner calling to serve, always amazed me. The only time I knew of him turning down work was when he was on vacation; otherwise, he was always available, even if it was miles away. He did say that the long-distance rides were lonely when I wasn't able to ride with him, but he always persevered anyway.

Life with Bob, and in this business, was a great adventure, to say the least, but some of these encounters were not a piece of cake. One certainly had to use intelligence and caution when dealing with many customers' situations. When Bob arrived on the scene, he would quiz the people to see if their story seemed legitimate. You never knew if someone was up to no good by trying to break in, and Bob always seemed to be able to test them by asking just the right questions. Because of his jovial attitude, he never seemed to offend, unless someone was doing something illegal, and the honest people really did appreciate him taking the time to investigate.

Sometimes meeting the customer was a surprise in itself. Once a call came in from a man who said in a delightfully peppy voice, "Hi, this is Fran Tarkenton. Can you help me?" He was a famous pro football quarterback in the NFL for the Minnesota Vikings and New York Giants in the sixties and seventies and later inducted into the Hall of Fame in 1986.[1]

I quickly replied, also in a peppy voice, "Hi, this is Kim from B & T Lock & Key. Yes, we can help you! What do you need?" We both burst into laughter, and I proceeded with the call.

There was always a story behind every encounter, and after coming to the caller's rescue, we had usually made a new friend. Bob's personality made his business even better. He never met a stranger, and his spirit was always up, no matter the time of day. He loved life and people with all of his heart, and serving was always foremost on his mind. He even called the local 911 authorities to offer his services for free in any situation needing an emergency rescue. No matter what the encounter, he couldn't help but leave you with a smile and serve you up some wit.

Speaking of wit, two nudist colonies in the area allowed for some on-the- job comedy. As you can imagine, since they didn't wear clothes, they were always needing our services. One very cold wintry night, a call came in to go to their clubhouse. Bob wondered if they were going to be wearing clothes since it was such a frigid night. As he anxiously traveled down the country road leading to the nudist camp, he watched with apprehension as he approached the clubhouse parking lot. Much to his surprise, the customer and the guests were wearing clothes. When he shared his thoughts with the customer, the customer playfully said, "We may be nudists, but did you think we were stupid?"

Another comical situation happened when a woman locked herself out of her car. Bob arrived on the scene and had her car unlocked so fast that she turned and instantly locked it back again, slamming the door shut. She said, "I want to see you do that again!"

Bob swiftly replied, "That'll be another forty-five dollars," and then said, "Just kidding!" They both burst into laughter. He did unlock the door once more, and they both continued to laugh.

Bob was so unpretentious. He believed people were the heartbeat of his company, and he treated them as such, with a smile thrown in for good measure.

Bob playing with brother, Chuckie

Bob playing cowboys

Bob swinging in Florida

**Bob and Kim, newly married,
Fort Lauderdale, Florida, 1974**

Bob and Kim, 1984

At cabin in Helen, Georgia, 2003

CHAPTER 2

The Day of Bad News

It was late September 2003 and not long after celebrating our business's ten-year anniversary. We were capturing a moment in time, looking out over our front yard and thinking about our approaching twenty-ninth wedding anniversary. We had literally grown up together, and we loved each other so much. As I had my arms around Bob's waist, I felt a quarter-size, rock-hard knot in his midstomach area just under the skin. I said, "What is that? You need to get that checked out!" Of course, being a typical man, he said, "No, it's all right." After another prompting, he finally agreed to go to our local family doctor, and an appointment was scheduled for the following week.

This doctor had used our locksmith services several times and had a good relationship with Bob. After they exchanged stories, the doctor proceeded with some questions. I then realized that Bob had lost a little weight and had been feeling a little fuller after eating. He, too, had recently wondered why he had been eating only half-portion sizes. For years Bob had dealt with indigestion, often taking antacids and on occasion "the purple pill." We just figured his indigestion problems were due to eating so late because of the locksmith lifestyle we lived.

Your body actually needs several hours to digest your food before you lie down at night. When you are sleeping, your body needs to be able to use its energy for rejuvenating your cells rather than digesting food that is in the stomach. Since Bob did not smoke, drink, or ever get sick, he assumed he was in great health. He thought, because he had turned fifty that year, that he was just going through some body changes. After the doctor finished his examination, he suggested Bob could have a hernia, but that he should schedule an appointment with a surgeon for a second opinion. He made the appointment, and we were worked in within a week.

Months before that, Bob's navel had begun to protrude a little more than usual. One day we got a service call to our rental cabin in Helen. It was a physician who just wanted a quick weekend reprieve. He had inadvertently locked his keys in his car, so he called our business for service. After Bob unlocked his car, they made small talk, and Bob asked if he was enjoying his stay at the cabin, telling him that we owned it. The doctor emphatically said, "I love it here, especially being right on the river."

The Chattahoochee River was so pristine and crystal clear as it approached from the bend and snaked past the cabin, allowing you to see every detail of its river bottom. The cabin had a large deck and boardwalk on the back, affording you privacy to enjoy every vantage point as the river traveled its path. The river contained a deep, aqua blue hole in the bend, perfect for fishing, since the Department of Natural Resources stocked the river there; it also had a shallow section perfect for wading, which was followed by a section of boulders that forced the swiftly flowing water into white water as the river descended its way into the tourist town of Helen. The sight of it all captured your attention, bringing pure enjoyment and peace.

He and Bob continued talking about the surrounding beauty, and Bob asked, "Since you are a doctor, would you mind looking at something?" The doctor said, "Sure!" and Bob quickly lifted his shirt and inquired if the doctor thought anything was unusual about his navel because of its recent protrusion. In retrospect, this was out of character for Bob, and it showed a concern more than he was willing to let on. The doctor made light of it, but did suggest he have it checked out. Bob, not liking to go to the doctor, thought he would just keep an eye on it. When he would speak of this protrusion, he would say, "I have an outie now," a clever play on words suggesting he meant an Audi car.

The following week we arrived at the surgeon's office. After the examination, he ordered tests from Bob's neck to his groin area: chest X-rays, CT scans of the abdomen and pelvis, an ultrasound of the gallbladder, and blood work. I was literally dumbfounded as he ordered the tests, and I knew that this was certainly not normal. Bob tended to make light of it; all the while, I think he knew that there was more to this than the doctor was letting on. Of course, the doctor couldn't say until he had the test results in hand.

We returned the following week for the results. The doctor had been on emergency-room call at Northeast Georgia Medical Center, and he had just treated several family members in a fatal car crash. We waited in the exam room a very long time before he finally entered, and when he did, it was with great sadness. He appeared as white as a ghost and zapped of all energy. He explained why he was late and apologized. After hearing his dreadful story, I figured his demeanor was just due to his recent experience, so my mind relaxed a bit, expecting to hear a good report from Bob's test results. But my hope quickly faltered as his solemn body language and facial expression did not change as he sat down to discuss the results. I realized something was terribly wrong.

At that moment, my heart began to pound. Fear consumed my mind, but then I dismissed my worry, thinking he might tell us another detail of his emergency-room experience. In the next second, the verdict was delivered. With a stoic look, he paused, and with great apprehension, he searched for strength to say what he was about to say. With a cracked voice, he said, "Mr. and Mrs. Doke, I have no good news for you."

He then asked if we wanted to see the X-rays and scans that were posted in the hallway outside. We nodded our heads in assent, stood up, grabbed each other's hands, and braced ourselves to see the results. Before we exited the room to look at the reports, the doctor said that they showed a 9 x 17 x 12 centimeter (3.5 x 6.7 x 4.7 inch) mass in Bob's stomach that originated from the stomach lining and that about 40 percent of his liver (both right and left lobes) was sporadically covered with cancerous cells as well. Because the cancer was in two different areas of the body, Bob was already at stage 4, the most advanced stage, for which there is usually no cure, but remissions are possible. The surgeon said the next step was to get biopsies from both the stomach and the liver cancer cells to determine the site of origination and to diagnose the exact type of cancer to know how to treat it. This would also confirm if the cancers in both areas were indeed the same cancer cells, that the cancer had metastasized and that there were not two different types of cancer.

We felt as if our hearts had been pierced. We clasped each other's hands for support. We knew that we were truly in God's hands and had no other options. It was the most helpless feeling I had ever felt, aside from experiencing a debilitating motorcycle accident several years earlier.

Cancer is staged in varying degrees from stage 1 to stage 4. There is usually no cure for stage 4, even though remission can be obtained. These stages have an important role in determining the most effective treatment. Staging is determined by the site of the primary tumor and the cell type, size of the tumor, involvement of regional lymph nodes and whether it has spread to distant sites, number of tumors, and tumor grade (how closely the cancer cells and tissue resemble normal cells and tissue).[2]

When we left his office, we were in a state of shock. That drive home will forever be embedded in my mind. Bob had driven our company van, thinking he might catch a call if needed after our appointment, but we were dumbfounded, and there were long periods of silence. No call would be serviced that hour or day. Bob's voice began to crack as he said, "I can't believe it. I just can't believe it! You always think this won't happen to you."

So many things were flying through my mind before and after Bob said that. I wondered, *What is going through his mind after receiving a diagnosis like that? How would I feel if I had just received the same news? How is he managing to continue to drive? What should I say? What can I say? Who should I call? Who should I call first?* I couldn't seem to get a grip on my thoughts. It was difficult to harness them. We both stared out the window for extended moments of time, privately dealing with the ravaging pain of it all.

Then I quickly thought about the Lord and how He was looking down on us. I wondered what He was thinking about how we were handling this. I thought about a scripture in Colossians 3:2: "Set your mind on things above, not on things on the earth." It was then that I needed to apply my reasoning to all that I had learned in my walk with the Lord: "I have set the Lord continually before me; because He is at my right hand, I will not be shaken" (Psalm 16:8, NASB).

I regained my composure, came back to reality, and realized that we did not have to be shaken by this. The Lord knew everything we were going through, even at that moment, and He would be with us through it all. We continued our drive home in a state of bewilderment, making phone calls to close family members and friends as they awaited the results of our doctor's visit.

CHAPTER 3

Carrots, Carrots, and More Carrots!

The next day, after the initial shock, I made a phone call to a friend who had her certificate in homeopathic health care through Hallelujah Acres in Shelby, North Carolina. She had been educating the public, along with the body of Christ (the church), for quite a while about health, diet, and disease. She also had a nursing degree and knew a good bit about medical terms and conditions. When I told her our diagnosis and what we were facing, I knew she knew that we were in for a vigorous battle. She suggested we come over immediately and that Bob begin to fill his body with living food. She urged us to give it our very best. She also offered to loan us her Champion juicer and suggested we start juicing carrots right away, along with any other fruits and vegetables.

I also purchased everything she thought Bob should be taking, such as Barley Green, Fiberblend, probiotics, enzymes, Udo's Choice Oil, and a myriad of pamphlets and books on health to try to get as much education and living food into Bob as possible. Being in a state of hopelessness, we both were willing to do whatever we could, within reason.

We loaded up the car and proceeded to stop at the local vegetable market where they sold organic produce. We bought the biggest bag of organic carrots they sold, a twenty-five-pound bag, to be exact! Bob had a look on his face of pure dread, but he was willing, if it would help buy him some time or perhaps even save his life. Since we arrived home around dinnertime, I decided I would jump on the bandwagon and start juicing right away, as time was of the essence. I had always tried to eat healthfully, but after what I had learned through this trial, I knew that I had a long way to go.

After wading through the endless amount of carrot waste, extracting enough juice to fill up our glasses, we tasted our first sample with great anticipation. It really wasn't what we thought it would taste like at all. In fact, I was pleasantly surprised! Bob wasn't doing somersaults, because he was a meat-and-potatoes guy, but he did give it his best and managed to get it down in intermittent gulps.

I decided that if he was going to experience a changed diet, then so would I. I was in it with him. Even though I had tried to eat a healthful diet, I had never juiced, only sampling a taste here and there at a friend's house or at a Whole Foods store. We couldn't help but chuckle, both of us downing the mixture of carrot juice; yet in the wake of our dilemma, I wondered how long Bob would be able to continue doing this. My friend had given me a regimen of what, how, and when Bob was supposed to eat, drink, and take these nutrients and juice. As Bob pondered the intense detailed schedule I had made, he looked dejected, hoping he would be able to press on with the diligence he knew he needed, but knowing it would be without cooperation from his taste buds or stomach.

After doing much research on the Internet, I read where it was suggested that diet has a significant impact on the development of stomach cancer. Studies showed that a high intake of foods traditionally preserved, salted, or pickled increases the risk of stomach cancer, while a diet rich in fruits and vegetables decreases that risk.[3] Bob loved smoked sausage, and on our way home from our Christmas vacation, we would always stop at a famous smokehouse south of Atlanta, where we would buy about ten pounds of smoked sausage. He loved to cook up several pounds and play a belated Santa Claus, visiting his business friends and acquaintances with the delivery of freshly cooked sausage. It thrilled him to be able to bless them, and I think he best loved the looks on their faces as he hit them with the element of surprise.

The juicing and extreme health plan went on for another two weeks until one afternoon when Bob came walking through the door as I had just juiced another big, bright, beautiful glass of carrot juice. He said to me, "Honey, I can't take it anymore!" I finally realized, despite my relentless desire and effort to cure my husband through diet, he was not going to go down that path anymore. He had decided to follow the medical path and that path alone. I, with what I call wisdom from the Lord, realized that trying to be a Proverbs 31 wife meant I needed to meet my husband where he was and respect his wishes. And that was not going to be with homeopathic methods. He had made up his mind, and I needed to rally with him.

That is what is so truly awesome about the Lord God. He meets us wherever we are in our faith journey, loving us tenderly all along the way. Romans 12:3 explains, "God has allotted to each a measure of faith" (NASB). And Psalm 16:5–6 says, "The Lord is the portion of my inheritance and my cup; You support my lot. The lines have fallen to me in pleasant places; indeed, my heritage is beautiful to me" (NASB).

CHAPTER 4

Pressing On for an Answer

~◎~

The following week we went for the CT-guided core biopsy of both the liver and the abdominal mass. A needle was inserted into the cancerous areas, and a core sample of the tumor tissue was extracted for further diagnosis. Unfortunately for Bob, the liver-biopsy test had to be repeated. After finally getting the results, we were once again greeted with bad news. It was another reality check that our lives were literally in God's hands.

This time the news reported that Bob's cancer was a very rare one, a sarcoma, called leiomyosarcoma, also known as LMS, which is an extremely rare and aggressive cancer and is very resistant to treatment.[4] The biopsies showed the tumor was negative for C-kit, confirming it was a metastatic spindle-cell neoplasm, consistent with LMS (C-kit, also called CD117, is a stem-cell-factor receptor and a type of tumor marker). Measuring the amount of C-kit in tumor tissue may help diagnose cancer and plan treatment.[5] The biopsy report also confirmed that the cancer cells in the liver were indeed the same as those cancerous cells in the lining of the stomach.

Only four in every million people have LMS.[6] The fact that it was a rare kind of cancer and that it had metastasized greatly limited our treatment options. Radiation or chemotherapy drugs had not been proven effective for this type of cancer. As a result, little funding had been given to researching this cancer to try and find a cure.[7] Companies do not want to exhaust their funds researching less common cancers, but invest in studies that bring results.

We knew then that Bob's situation did not make him a candidate for any type of possible remission. We asked the doctor how long he thought Bob had to live, based on his condition and past cases of this cancer type; he said six to twelve months. My body felt a warm rush as fear enveloped me. Bob's look affirmed he did too. *What? Are you serious?* Our whole lives changed in one instant. Countless thoughts flooded my mind, as I know they did Bob's, wondering how long we really did have and how our lives would actually play out.

LMS is actually a rare soft-tissue sarcoma cancer. These are cancers where wildly growing (malignant, or cancerous) cells originate from a soft tissue in the body. All cancers start from one particular cell that mutates. Its DNA is damaged by mutations and changes so that the cell no longer grows in an orderly fashion as God determined it. The cancer is often named for the cell type that it grows from, but sometimes it has other names.

The soft tissues of the body include fat, blood vessels, nerves, muscles, skin, and cartilage. You have essentially two kinds of muscles in your body: voluntary and involuntary. The body's muscular system is composed of both smooth and striated (striped) muscle cells. Smooth muscle cells make up the involuntary muscles that are found in most parts of the body: the uterus, stomach and intestines, walls of all blood vessels, and skin (goose bumps). Striated muscle cells make up the voluntary muscles: the biceps, triceps, abs, pectorals—all the muscles you choose to move.[8]

Since Bob's stomach tumor was in the smooth muscle cells that were in the lining of his stomach, there was no way to remove the tumor without removing his whole stomach. You can live without a stomach, but your quality of life is highly compromised. Removing the stomach might have been a possibility had the cancer not metastasized to the liver. A liver transplant might have been an option had there not been cancer in the stomach lining. Bob was in a catch-22 situation; any solution for one organ was denied because of the presence of the other affected organ.

After our discussion with the surgeon, he said he would need to refer us to an oncologist for ongoing care and palliative treatment. He gave us the names of oncology doctors in town. We were once again filled with a heaviness of heart, not knowing what the future held, whether we would choose experimental treatments if any were available, or how we would decide to live out the remainder of Bob's life. So many things were unknown. Our world had turned totally upside down during that three-week period, and the news was getting worse with every step of our journey.

A flurry of things was now running through our minds. The primary thought was, *What do we do now that we have been given this short life sentence?* Should we plan a wonderful trip and try to take in all the beauty of life, doing things we put off because we had worked so hard growing our business, or should we go on a fabulous vacation to a faraway place? Should we sell our primary house and move to the new cabin we had just built as an investment on the Chattahoochee River in downtown Helen, Georgia? Should we throw all caution to the wind and celebrate life in general, or should we think logically, not do anything irrational, and keep living life as we had before?

Another question we considered was whether we should sell our locksmith business. I'm sure Bob was thinking, *I've worked so hard to grow it. What if I sell and then get healed? My business will be sold, and then what will I do?*

After the jumble of all the "I don't knows," fears, concerns, and questions, we did know one thing: the Lord was on our side. I said, "You know, Bob, we win either way. We win in life, and we win in death." I thought, *Either I believe the Bible or I don't! I am now in a position to prove what I believe. I believe that the blood of Jesus Christ has conquered sin, spiritual death, and the grave! When we understand our need for a Savior, we are given the Holy Spirit to help us overcome sin and give us eternal life. That means our spirits will live on in eternity, and we will get to spend eternity together.*

After that, Bob and I were resolved to live by our belief and faith in God and fight this battle with confidence and tenacity. Psalm 138:3 says, "On the day I called, You answered me; You made me bold with strength in my soul" (NASB). We proceeded with boldness of strength, fighting with all our might with God on our side. We saw our fight with cancer as a farmer who toils with a plow, furrowing a row of hope for the next person or generation who would be dealing with this kind of cancer. We were blazing a trail for the Lord's glory! We knew that whether He healed Bob or not, we would choose to serve Him because He is faithful, and we knew He would be with us through it all.

The Lord says through the prophet in Jeremiah 17:7–8, "Blessed is the man who trusts in the Lord, and whose trust is the Lord. For he will be like a tree planted by the water, that extends its roots by a stream and will not fear when the heat comes; but its leaves will be green, and it will not be anxious in a year of drought nor cease to yield fruit" (NASB). How incredible to know that even in our trial, because we were trusting in the Lord, we could still produce fruit! The Lord God had given us a peace that the world didn't understand. It was a perfect peace that was deep in our souls and could come only from Him. I had seen the Lord's mighty hand in our lives so many times before, evidence of His wonder-working power; I was not about to begin to walk by my flesh now, giving up my faith. Walking by faith is to trust that wherever your circumstances take you, you win either way. You win if God performs a miracle and you get to give Him the glory, and you win if you die because He promises to receive you in glory.

I originally gave my life to the one whose image I am made in, the Lord God and His Son Jesus Christ, in my preteens; Bob had given his life as a young boy. We both started neglecting our relationship with the Lord in our late teens as we sought the ways of the world. After having a motorcycle wreck in August of 1990 and realizing just how fragile life was, I rededicated my life to the Lord. Bob did not rededicate his life at that time.

Not long after this, I was reading my Bible and came across a scripture in 1 Corinthians 7:14. It said the unbelieving husband is sanctified through his wife, and the unbelieving wife is sanctified through her believing husband. Even though Bob did not fully unite with me in my Christian walk, he never asked to be released from our marriage. I pondered the depth of that scripture, figuring that because the Holy Spirit dwelled in me and I dwelled in my home, my husband could not help but be influenced by God's presence. I had to stand on God's promises because I specifically witnessed God's work through Bob on several occasions.

One day Bob was talking with a customer who was sharing his personal problems with him. Bob simply stated, "I'll ask my wife to pray for you." Another fruit of God's sanctifying work was when a church called to rekey their premises. Upon finishing the job, Bob tallied the bill. Then, on the bottom line, he put a big zero and said, "Paid in full. Happy birthday—Jesus." Even though Bob was not shy and was fairly outgoing, he was not boastful about his actions that day, actions that clearly displayed the underlying work of the Holy Spirit in his life. When I asked, "How much did you charge them?" he sheepishly slid the "paid in full" bill over to me and looked away, not saying a word.

Another proof of God's sanctifying work in him was when he placed an order for key blanks to stock his inventory. The company he ordered from would inscribe on both sides of the key blank, and initially, Bob had put our company name on one side and his friend's company on the other. A few years later, he nonchalantly walked across our driveway, holding out a key blank and said, "Do you want to see my new blanks?"

As I reached out to receive it, my face revealed my puzzled thought, *Hmm, what's this all about?* As I looked closer, I saw that it had our company name, but a new impression on the back side. It said "WWJD & John 3:16." WWJD is an acronym that started in the nineties and means "What would Jesus do?" Was I surprised, and all along my heart was exploding with thankfulness to the Lord! I said to Bob, "Wow, that's nice!"

As I pondered this in my heart, I began to think about Mary, in Luke 2, when the shepherds visited her after Jesus was born. The Bible says Mary pondered the things the shepherds told her: that angels had visited them and told them of the Christ child, confirming that God was a God of promise. I went away that day grateful, pondering God's wonder and power as He worked in my husband's heart.

The day we received the news that Bob's cancer was terminal only served to remind me that life on this earth is in God's timing, not mine. There is power in my hands, but only to act as His servant while He fulfills His plan, even in the pain. I knew that our Savior and Lord had never left us, and He wasn't about to leave us now! Deuteronomy 31:6 says, "Be strong and courageous, do not be afraid or tremble at them, for the Lord your God is the one who goes with you. He will not fail you or forsake you" (NASB). Even though I didn't fully understand, I knew He would bring glory in it; I knew He could take what the enemy meant for harm and turn it for the good (see Genesis 50:20). This trial would allow Him to show up, to be seen, for His glory to be displayed.

We decided to take a weekend vacation with the family before scheduling an appointment with the oncologist. As our family heard of Bob's news, there was a silent camaraderie, a knitting of souls that began to form. It was like we didn't have to speak a word; we silently knew that we loved each other tremendously, and we knew we would be there for each other through the thick and thin of this ordeal. We planned a family weekend getaway; and we rented a seventeen-passenger van so we could all spend some time together. Since it was late October and fall was nearly spent, it was a perfect time to unite and catch one more glimpse of fall in her fading glory.

One by one our family arrived. My brother and his family drove up from Florida, and my parents and Bob's mom joined us, since they lived nearby. We decided to go to the beautiful town of Saluda, North Carolina, a historic Victorian town at the foot of the Blue Ridge Mountains. It is a place with quaint little shops and restaurants and views of fall-splashed hues on the surrounding mountains. Saluda is one of western North Carolina's hidden beauties. We also visited Carl Sandburg's home, Connemara, in Flat Rock, North Carolina. He was a great American poet, journalist, historian, biographer, and autobiographer.[9] After a great day of visiting Saluda and touring Sandburg's home place, we made our way back home to Cleveland, Georgia, for the night.

The next day we decided to take one last drive north through the familiar north Georgia mountains' apple country before everyone headed home. We wanted to travel the familiar roads together once again, capturing one last glimpse of the season's display of color. Several of us had taken this route many times before in the peak of apple season, stopping at all the cider houses; drinking fresh, cold apple cider; sampling and buying freshly picked apples; and, of course, sampling those famous hot french-fried apple-cider donuts. The day was a rainy one, and the terrain was wet and glistening, but it did not stop us from venturing out; after all, we were on a mission to knit our hearts and souls together.

Since the weekend trip was nearing its end and we knew our time spent together would be coming to a close, everyone's mood was turning a little somber. After driving through the mountains for several hours, we began to make our way back to Cleveland. The journey home seemed as if it were momentarily frozen in time. Each of us seemed to be bound within our mind, deep in thought. It seemed as if we were trying to enjoy the silent beauty of the moment, trying to apprehend and cherish the memories of the day at hand with Bob; yet we were sorrowful, knowing the odds. Would he live six months, twelve months? If not, then how many? We didn't want the day to end, and each of us was wondering how many more times we would have together.

CHAPTER 5

In the Hands of a Doctor

The next week we selected an oncologist in Gainesville, Georgia, and made the first available appointment on October 23, 2003. After the doctor reviewed the scans and reports, we all had a very candid discussion about Bob's diagnosis and treatment options for this very rare cancer. The doctor let us know that we needed to get our personal and business affairs in order if we hadn't already. He said the statistics of survival were about six months to a year, as we had already been told. He suggested we apply for Social Security disability because of Bob's expected life span, and then he proceeded to write this letter:

To Whom It May Concern:

Mr. Doke is currently under my care for metastatic gastric leiomyosarcoma, diagnosed 10/10/03. This is a type of cancer for which there is no cure and an expected survival of only 6–12 months. Due to his cancer and treatment, it is neither safe nor feasible for him to work or do work-related

activities. Please extend all possible cour-
tesies to Mr. Doke with respect to disability
benefits during this difficult time.

Sincerely,
Doctor _____

Receiving this advice and letter just added to the
heavy cloud that was already over us, but we followed
the doctor's advice and applied for Social Security benefits right away. We heard that it usually takes several
tries before receiving approval. We were also told that it
would take six months before we would draw the first
payment. At the same time, we wondered if it was worth
filing for; would Bob still be around to collect it?

Already having a business mind-set, we had our
wills, living wills, and legal affairs in order. We called
our attorney to tell him the bad news and to see if there
were any additional legal steps we needed to take. He
suggested we switch from a living will to a durable power
of attorney for health care. This was a very valuable and
crucial step. Because we were dealing with a fatal diagnosis, this would allow Bob to proceed with any kind
of experimental treatment and also give his doctor lib-
erty. With our living will, Bob had indicated DNR (do
not resuscitate). As a result of this, he would not have
had the option for resuscitation or any life-sustaining
methods. Since he wanted to pursue any medical path
available, his living will could have been a catch 22 for
him, blocking any advancement.

A living will or advance directive speaks for you without
the availability of appeal. It is a legal document that has
been properly witnessed by an authority (notary), and
it allows you to state, in writing, your wishes or refusal
for treatment by artificial means, heroic measures, even
for food and water. It is a legally recognized statement
upheld in court. If you decide to prepare a living will, be

sure to talk with your doctor or lawyer to identify and define the terms that will be important to your future medical care, such as *artificial means, heroic measures,* and *code status.*

A durable power of attorney for health care is different. Treatments can be considered at the time of need with your doctor and the one to whom you have given power of attorney. The named power of attorney on the document does not mean an actual attorney, but can be any layperson of your choosing, one whom you trust to make life-and-death decisions regarding your health care, who knows how you feel about specific treatments, and who is familiar with your religious beliefs and wishes.[10]

In a case where you are fighting for your life, you certainly need your legal affairs to line up with your wishes. If Bob had not switched to the durable power of attorney for health care, it would have tied the doctors' and health-care providers' hands for any experimental treatments he might want. We were engaged in a battle for Bob's life, and the last thing we wanted was to prohibit his progress. This document also proved to be beneficial, as Bob was determined to fight his battle to the end, having several procedures and major surgery.

Next, our oncology doctor made a phone call to an oncologist in Atlanta, Georgia, inquiring if there were any clinical trials going on for sarcomas. The reply was no. It was another roadblock that took our hope. "Hope deferred makes the heart sick, but when the desire comes, it is a tree of life" (Proverbs 13:12). Any hope we had was taking flight. It was just another opportunity to remember whose hands we were really in and to cling to Him.

My mind was filled with a ton of questions. In a frantic tone, I asked the doctor, "Aren't there any other facilities, cancer hospitals, or drug companies in the country, in the world, doing any type of treatment, experimental or otherwise, that we can go to?" We were desperate and frantically searching for anything available. The doctor halfheartedly replied that we could seek out one of the top cancer hospitals in the nation to see if they had any clinical trials going on. I think he answered halfheartedly because he knew the odds were against us.

The doctor stepped out of the room to call MD Anderson Cancer Center in Houston, Texas. They were ranked by *U.S. News and World Report* as one of the top-two cancer hospitals in the world.[11] After several minutes, he entered the room, only to tell us they did not have any current trials, but that we could schedule an appointment for an evaluation. I didn't understand why we had to travel there for an evaluation when he had all our records and could just relate our situation. I thought Bob's case could be discussed over the phone, and then, if there were any possibilities of a clinical trial or treatment option, we would go. But our oncologist stated that protocol was to set up an appointment to be evaluated first. We both wanted to go but were puzzled at how the whole ordeal had to be handled, not fully under-standing why they couldn't discuss our case first to see if Bob might be a candidate before making the long trip. Since we had run out of options locally, we decided to let the doctor make the appointment referring us for an evaluation.

We took the first available appointment—December 29, 2003—and planned our Christmas vacation around it. We would spend time with my family in Quincy, Florida, and then leave for Houston the day after Christmas. We figured the drive to Houston would be about two to three days from my brother's house, and since we needed to head south to take I-10 to Houston anyway, it worked out perfectly to leave from there. For the moment, every-thing seemed to be lining up, even though this Christmas would be like none we had ever celebrated, our hearts heavy and burdened by Bob's diagnosis. We wondered, would this be the last Christmas, or would there be another? With every decision we made, questions flew through my mind and reminded me just how much I desperately wanted to know the future—Bob's future!

After our oncology doctor spoke with the oncologist in Houston, both doctors recommended that before going to MD Anderson, Bob start with a combination chemotherapy treatment of gemcitabine (Gemzar) and Taxotere. Our oncology doctor explained that the administration of this combination might be associated with a 30–50 percent response rate in nonuterine leiomyosarcomas. This did not mean it was a cure, but only that if we did fall into this possible percentile, it would stun the cancer cells and perhaps buy us some time. Before we went to MD Anderson, the doctor wanted to try this for two successive rounds, and he wanted to perform a scan after the treatments to see if the chemo had worked. So we scheduled an appointment for the first round of chemotherapy.

Bob braved it with little apprehension, knowing he really had no other options. He felt that it was better to have tried and failed than not to have tried at all. We literally knew nothing about chemotherapy, but after arriving for Bob's first scheduled dose and searching on the Internet, I learned more than I wanted. I could tell by Bob's subtle responses and behavior that he didn't want to know how it worked; he just wanted to get started. He was content to completely trust the doctor's advice.

When Bob was diagnosed, I had no idea what cancer was. I searched the Internet, asking, "What is cancer?" and I clicked on an interesting link called www.cancer-help.org.uk/help (October 2003). It's now known as www.cancerresearchuk.org/cancer-help/about-cancer/what-is-cancer/cells/the-cancer-cell (2014). I discovered that a normal cell has receptors, and when its surface loses its molecules, it becomes defective, not allowing the cell to communicate with other cells. Because of its defectiveness, the cell doesn't fulfill its functional purpose or stay in its intended place. The defective cell stops obeying signals from other neighboring good cells. It becomes detached from the good cells and carries on reproducing in its abnormal way. It travels throughout the body where it doesn't belong, not dying when it becomes defunct. And cancer cells don't ever become specialized, but stay immature. They stop doing the job that God purposed them to.

As I read this wealth of information, I was reminded of the scripture in Romans 1:20 of how everything in nature, in the tangible realm, reveals who God is—His invisible attributes, eternal power, and divine nature. Since God is revealed in all of nature, why not in the stages of a cell? He made them!

When I saw this cell explanation, I immediately saw it applied to the body of Christ, the church. Normal healthy cells represent the body of Christ—how we as believers are to be:

1. A normal cell is made to reproduce itself exactly and carry on reproducing in the fashion it was created to. We as Christians are to become disciples and are to make disciples.
2. A normal cell is to stop its reproductive behavior at the right time. We are to stop certain behavior at the correct time. If directed by family, friends, leadership, or clergy, we should consider and honor their wisdom, as long as it's measured using God's Word, and stop our identified action or behavior. We also need to recognize and respect seasons and times for specific ministries that need to come to an end.
3. Normal or healthy cells are to stick together in the appropriate place. We are to stick together in the proper place, time, and season, using our gifts and talents, encouraging and helping one another in the body of Christ.

4. A normal cell should self-destruct when it is damaged. We should "self-destruct" when we are damaged (hurt, wounded, or offended), meaning we should crucify our flesh when required (Mark 8:34), allow our offenses to fall on Christ (Romans 15:3), and forgive others or ask for forgiveness when necessary (Mark 11:25–26).

5. And lastly, a normal cell becomes specialized or mature. As we walk by faith with the Lord, we are to grow to become specialized, allowing Him to take us from faith to glory, becoming mature disciples. How amazing that the life of a healthy single cell parallels God's perfect design for the body of Christ!

When a cell goes awry or becomes defective, it will carry on reproducing. So it is that when someone has been hurt, they further wound the body of Christ and influence others to join in their cause. They don't self-discipline or crucify their flesh (self-destruct) when they are damaged, but they multiply their defectiveness further. They don't stop reproducing their hurt, bitterness, and anger. They don't stay in one place, but move to another part of the body, taking their sin, hurtful words, and destructive works with them. And they don't mature or become specialized in any area, but stay immature.

Cancer cells do just the opposite of healthy or normal cells. They do not stop producing after they have doubled fifty or sixty times. They will go on and on doubling. One cell becomes two, two becomes four, four becomes eight, eight becomes sixteen, and so on.[12] Oh, what a lesson seen in the physical realm, which reveals a spiritual truth! Just as the life of a healthy cell can be viewed through the lens of God's creation (the law of the Spirit of life), a defunct cell represents the fall of man (the law of sin and death) as described in Romans 8:2.

Because cancer cells grow and divide more rapidly than normal cells, many anticancer drugs are made to kill the growing cells. And because certain normal, healthy cells also multiply quickly, chemotherapy can affect these cells too. This damage to normal cells is actually what causes the side effects.

The fast-growing normal cells most likely to be affected are blood cells forming in the bone marrow and cells in the digestive tract (mouth, stomach, intestines, esophagus), reproductive system (sexual organs), and hair follicles. Some anticancer drugs may affect cells of vital organs such as the heart, kidney, bladder, lungs, and nervous system, and on some occasions, they can cause permanent changes or damage to these organs. Certain chemotherapy drugs may also have delayed effects, such as a second cancer that may show up years later.[13] Even though this is very disheartening, you must weigh your concerns with the immediate threat of your cancer and the treatment's ability to destroy it.

There has been great progress made in preventing and treating some of chemotherapy's side effects. Many new drugs and treatment methods destroy cancer more effectively while doing less harm to the body's healthy cells. The doctor's office can give you resource materials to help you better understand everything you will need to know. When taking chemotherapy drugs, you may not have any of the side effects, or just a few. The severity of these side effects depends on the type and dose of chemotherapy you receive and how your body reacts to it. The initial condition of your health can also make a huge difference in your response. Before starting any treatment, the doctor will discuss the options with you, and then you may be asked to sign a consent form. You should be given all the facts before receiving treatment or signing any consent forms, including the drugs you will be given and their side effects.

The whole ordeal of the chemotherapy procedure was equivocal to a hurt child looking up to his parent in total dependency, and that is the stance Bob took with his doctor. He totally trusted and depended on him.

The first round of chemotherapy was gemcitabine HCL, aka Gemzar, and in the beginning, there were a few manageable side effects. Bob's symptoms were fevers, sweats, constipation, and flulike symptoms. These were all noted in the chemotherapy guide as possible side effects. After the second week, Bob began to have more symptoms, such as a rash covering his entire stomach and oral sores. These too were noted as possible side effects. Even though dealing with these symptoms was alarming at first, and certainly a nuisance, they were tolerable with medicine.

Bob had always worn a full beard, but after a few weeks of chemo, the hair on his face, head, and body started to fall out. At first, it came out very gently, finding only a few hairs on his pillowcase or shirt collar. Then it began to fall out much more easily, almost as if the hair follicles had relaxed and were just barely holding on to the hair shaft at the root, waiting to be released. Since a buzz was in order, he delightfully donned his new do.

One day Bob walked up to me and playfully pinched a half inch of hair, pulling it out while simultaneously yelling, "Ouch!" His playful eyes and look gave him away as he said, "Ah ha, I gotcha!"

I quickly swatted at him, acknowledging his mischievousness and knowing it didn't really hurt like he had pretended. I shook my head, saying, "You're crazy!" After living with him, I should have known he would do something like that.

One day he came home and told me the story of a woman he had met and shared chemotherapy stories with. She told him she was walking across the street on her way to church when a big gust of wind came and blew most of her hair off her head. Because she had used hair spray, the wind picked up her hair and flung it like a flying saucer. I suppose it was quite a shock to her and to those who witnessed it. Her hair follicles must have been loose and ready to let go. She and Bob got a good laugh out of that. Bob never lost his sense of humor; he never let a moment go by without telling a funny story or pulling his hair out (when he had it) to play a trick on you.

Bob never let his storm take him down. He knew there was nothing he ultimately could do about it. He knew he was totally in God's care, so he decided to continue living life as large as he had before. He could choose to let this storm take him down by stealing his joy, peace, and strength, or he could decide to ride into that storm, letting the clouds take him higher. He wanted and purposed to give life all that he could as long as he could.

It was time for round two, and the name of this drug was docetaxel, aka Taxotere. The side effects Bob experienced with this drug were a little different. He suffered a sore neck, again flulike symptoms, diarrhea, and hives and blisters that covered his neck and chest. Decadron pills were given to take the day before he started chemotherapy and for five days after, which really helped reduce the nausea.

I had decided to have a cup of coffee with my friend Gloria. Bob was home watching his favorite television show, *Leave It to Beaver*, nestled in his favorite recliner. While gone, I called to check on him. Each time he said he was doing fine, so I stayed out a little longer, enjoying my time with Gloria, but also with the idea that I'd be going home to see Bob soon.

Upon returning home, I immediately walked to the family room where he was and saw that he had a concerned, fearful look on his face, which was unusual for him. He said, "My temperature is 102 degrees, and I'm sweating." A feeling of panic came over me as I fumbled to reread the doctor's instructions for which symptoms were normal and which were not. He had said to call his office if Bob's fever reached 102 or higher, so I decided to call and have him paged. I was informed that this was a normal reaction and to give him a fever reducer to try to bring his temperature down. It worked and brought much relief to our nerves. I later found out that a spiking fever was normal while on chemo and one of the many possible side effects. A fever could shoot up in half an hour with no warning whatsoever. So after that, I tried to never leave Bob for any unnecessary length of time, remaining by his side as much as I could. Bob continued to run his locksmith business, and I, for the time being, continued to work at my church as part-time staff.

After Bob's two cycles (two months) of chemo, the doctor scheduled his follow-up CT scan on December 9, 2003, to be compared to the original CT scan on October 9, 2003. The results showed that the large mass in his upper abdomen appeared to have increased somewhat since the previous examination, and the extent of metastatic disease in the liver had not significantly changed. This just confirmed that our planned visit to MD Anderson Cancer Center was in our best and only interest.

About two weeks prior to our trip to MD Anderson, my sister in-law, Mariam, happened to be reading the *Tallahassee Democrat* newspaper and saw an article about a new TomoTherapy machine that delivered low-dose radiation. It was at the Southeast Regional Cancer Center in Tallahassee, Florida, and had proven to be effective for sarcoma patients. According to the center's chairman, Dr. Eric Rost, the $3 million machine represented the future in the fight against cancer. In the article, Rost described how the TomoTherapy Hi-Art System used electric energy to locate and destroy cancer without harming the surrounding tissue and without the side effects associated with more traditional radiation and chemotherapy. The system was one of five in the world and had been on the market for about two years. The first four machines manufactured were in university settings, and the machine at Southeast Regional was the first machine used in a commercial setting.

The machine acts like a CT scanner to give physicians a three-dimensional view of all tissue in a cancer-affected area. A large drum rotates around the patient, who is conscious and not anesthetized for the painless procedure. A computer is used to determine the precise location of the cancer cells, and the computer then determines how to release short bursts of energy that destroy the cancer cells, but not healthy surrounding tissue. Because the machine can target more than one affected area, a patient with cancer in multiple parts of the body can receive treatment. Dr. Rost said the machine was capable of treating tumors previously considered inoperable or untreatable because of their location. "This can hit a field of (cells) with the most specificity in the world," he said, "without causing damage to any surrounding tissue."[14]

Mariam was elated as she called us, giving us this valuable information. As she talked, I felt excitement welling up in me and couldn't write the phone number down fast enough. I immediately thought, *How incredible if the doctor can fit us in when we go at Christmastime!* We had such a small window of time; the only days we had available were right before Christmas, since we were heading to Houston the day after. I quickly called to see if we could schedule an appointment, and by God's grace, we were able to get in exactly as needed, on December 23. Praise the Lord—great things He was doing!

CHAPTER 6

Life Goes On

~✎©~

We went about our business as usual, looking forward to our trip to Tallahassee and then to Houston, filled with anticipation that there might be something or someone still out there in this great big world who could help us. Even though you know the Lord is with you, you still cling to this tangible realm for help.

Bob continued to run his locksmith business with the same diligence as before, and I continued working at my church, but things were different now. Bob was telling everyone he met about his plight and asking if they wanted to buy his business. Despite this, he did not let his predicament allow him to skip a beat, pressing on with the same love for life and pleasant attitude he had before. In fact, the people he told his story to were in such disbelief of his diagnosis because he continued to display his jovial wit, contagious smile, and zest for life. Even though his overall attitude was still exuberant, I noticed that the happy-go-lucky part of him had retreated a little.

Bob was always willing to help people, especially young entrepreneurs, and he saw his predicament as a tool for others to learn from his experience. If he were going to go down, he would go down with purpose! He took every opportunity to tell people how important it was to have life and disability insurance. He wanted to help others so that they too, if ever found in his situation, would be prepared. He realized how easy it would be to lose everything you worked so hard for because of poor financial or legal planning. He valued the legal decisions he had made because they gave him peace of mind—peace to know that I could quit work to be home with him, that we could financially get through this trial, and that I would be taken care of if he died. We had always tried to be wise by having insurance coverage, but not to the extent of being what some call "insurance poor," where all your money is spent paying costly insurance premiums.

Not long after Bob started his business, he took out a disability policy because he, being the sole business owner, knew that if anything happened to him, there would be no income. He decided to take out a policy that had a one-year elimination period. That meant the insurance benefit would kick in after one year of being disabled. This kept our monthly premiums affordable, and we figured if anything did happen, we could make it a year living on our savings and by cutting out all luxuries. Since Bob was in great health and only thirty-nine years old at the time he started his business, most people wondered why he bothered getting disability insurance at all, but it sure proved to pay off when he was diagnosed with terminal cancer.

The policy promised to pay the difference of up to $2,500 a month, after Social Security disability. Because Bob's life expectancy was only six to twelve months, the insurance company waived the one-year waiting period and started paying after six months. What a relief, giving me the freedom and opportunity to quit work and concentrate on taking care of him, our needs and responsibilities, and living out our days together.

While I was at my church, my pastor happened to see me in the hall and asked how I was doing. I paused for a minute and replied, "I'm hanging in there." As soon as I said that, the Holy Spirit convicted me, but at that moment, I didn't know why.

My pastor looked at me with disbelief and replied, "Kim, you are not hanging in there. You are persevering with excellence!"

I quickly retorted, "You are right!" because I knew that the Lord was my strength and mighty fortress.

It wasn't until about a week later that the Lord showed me why I shouldn't have said that. He let me know that He didn't send His Son, Jesus Christ, to die on a cross just for me to "hang in there." I realized that with the Lord on our side, without a doubt we could persevere with excellence, the excellence that He promised in His Word. Isaiah 26:3–4 says, "The steadfast of mind You will keep in perfect peace, because he trusts in You. Trust in the Lord forever, for in God the Lord, we have an everlasting Rock" (NASB).

This reminds me of the eagle and how he responds to an approaching storm. Other birds sense the storm coming and head for cover, but not the mighty eagle. No, he literally sits on the edge of his nest, waiting expectantly for the storm. When it comes, he locks his wings in an ascending position and uses the storm's strong winds to help him spiral round and round, rising higher and higher until ultimately he begins to see sunlight around him and the storm below. He rides the storm until he rises above it.

God's Word reveals the picture of the eagle (Isaiah 40:31). The one who puts his hope in the Lord can soar like an eagle, even in a storm—especially in a storm! You have no choice about getting hit by the storm, and you certainly have no control over it, but you do have a choice about how you handle the storm. You can let it frighten you into retreating or giving up, you can let it consume you, or you can fly into that storm and let it take you higher than you have ever flown before.

Since radiation and chemotherapy had not proven to be effective on sarcomas, clinical trials were our only option; that is, if any were happening. Even though we had our upcoming appointment scheduled at MD Anderson Cancer Center and our appointment in Tallahassee with Dr. Rost, we knew that we needed to continue to aggressively search for any other treatment possibilities. Bob's family and I tenaciously began to search the Internet. Having a rare cancer puts you in an isolated yet unique position, one where you may have an opportunity to pioneer for a new treatment and help future cancer patients. Bob was willing to do almost anything.

I had never heard of a clinical trial before and knew absolutely nothing about them. After speaking with our doctor and researching on the Internet, I discovered that our efforts were futile because, at the time, there were no clinical trials or other treatment options available, with the exception of going to another country for a non-FDA-approved treatment.

For any treatment out of the country, there was much to be considered. Cost, for one, played a significant role; these treatments were not usually covered by a medical insurance company and would be totally out of pocket. Because they had no government regulation and no proven statistics, Bob was not willing to possibly exhaust our entire life savings. He wanted to protect and preserve what he had planned and worked so hard for, the future I would live after he was gone.

While researching clinical trials, we discovered they were divided into four categories from phase 1 to 4. Phase 1 is when new drugs are introduced to the human population via a small group of volunteering participants. This is to show that the drug is not toxic to humans. Phase 2 is when drugs are given to a larger group of participants to further evaluate their safety. Phase 3 is when drugs are given to large groups of people to confirm their effectiveness because phases 1 and 2 have already been completed. Phase 3 also monitors side effects and compares them to established FDA-approved treatments. Phase 4 is after the drug has reached the mainstream patient population and is FDA-approved. In this phase, studies are done, allowing further information to be collected to determine side effects of long-term use.[15]

Knowing all of this information, we felt more equipped than before to make our trek to MD Anderson. We knew we could now make an intelligent decision regarding how far we wanted to go with clinical trials; that is, if any became available. I told Bob that I personally would not want to do a clinical trial unless it was a phase 4 trial, but he would have to make that decision for himself. I said, "Whatever you decide, I will be behind you 100 percent." I knew then that I must be ready to go through uncharted territory with him, if that's what he decided.

CHAPTER 7

The Medical Trek

C hristmas was almost here, and it was time to prepare for our trip to Tallahassee and to Houston. As
the days quickly approached, there was a feeling of anxiety and anticipation as we readied ourselves to walk
in an unknown territory. The questions were endless.
We wondered, what medical options would be available?
What would our doctor be like? Would we see many doctors? Would we be treated like a specimen before a tumor
board? What was Houston like, and would it be easy to
find our way around? Could we possibly include some
fun while there? Would we end up staying longer than
anticipated for treatment or surgery, having to rent an
apartment like others we had talked to? How would we
run our business, rental properties, and affairs from
Houston if we did have to stay? Or would it be another
dead end?

We got our affairs in order, preparing to be gone for an
unknown amount of time that would be determined only
by the Lord and the doctors we were about to see. We
made sure we had all of Bob's medical records, including
CT scans, X-rays, labs, our referral letter from our oncologist, and, of course, all of our carefully hand-selected
Christmas gifts.

We headed out that morning for Tallahassee and realized we had cell-phone coverage only for the state of Georgia. We decided to stop at a Cingular office on our way out of town to change our cell-phone plan to one that would have service throughout the whole country. We wanted to be able to call family and friends from Houston without paying roaming fees and to plan for any other traveling we might do, God willing.

We arrived at my brother's house in Quincy a few days before Christmas, just in time to get settled in and make our scheduled appointment the following day with Dr. Rost. The evaluation with him was one of the most encouraging ones Bob had received, and it changed our whole outlook. He stated the grim diagnosis that we were certainly familiar with, but also offered a new regimen of treatments. He went on to say that he would approach Bob's diagnosis with all three multidisciplinary approaches: chemotherapy, surgery, and radiation with a new TomoTherapy machine that was being set up as we met. If we did go this route, he suggested we go to our oncologist in Georgia for the chemotherapy, come to him for the low-dose radiation (TomoTherapy) to target the liver cancer, and seek out a surgeon who would debulk Bob's stomach tumor.

He let us know that it would not be easy to find a surgeon to operate, but he would check with his associates to see if any were willing. Knowing we were on our way to MD Anderson, he strongly suggested that we urge the doctors there to operate. He knew if anyone would, they would. Because Bob's cancer had metastasized, there were no doctors, other than this one, who was offering anything other than palliative treatment.

A doctor's goal is to shoot for a cure, no matter how small, but in Bob's case, there was no cure as far as the medical field was concerned. We were told he couldn't receive stomach surgery (debulking) because of the liver cancer, and he couldn't receive a new liver because of the stomach cancer. But this doctor's suggestions for approaches had certainly given us more hope than ever before. Perhaps it was a false or limited hope, but to us, any hope was better than none.

Our attitudes certainly changed as our consultation progressed with Dr. Rost, and when we finally exited his office, Bob actually had a little spring back in his step. We felt as though the heavy weight that had been on us had taken flight and perched itself on a high and distant cloud, still there, but momentarily out of reach. This prospect gave us the lift we needed to be able to experience Christmas almost as joyfully as we had in the past.

The following few days at my brother's with his family and our parents were the best ever. While the light-hearted celebrations of the past were a memory, we were determined to celebrate, albeit in a much different way. We would hold on to each moment, each gesture, each smile, each comment, each story, each joke, not knowing if it would be the last, not knowing how many more we had, but knowing we would cherish each memory.

On Christmas Eve, we dressed in our Christmas best and headed for the service at my brother's church in Tallahassee. It had always been our tradition to go to the evening candlelight service and then return home to begin the Christmas festivities. My sister-in-law, Mariam, who is a great cook, labored in the kitchen for hours, preparing a myriad of festive dishes to be enjoyed at our leisure—recipes of spiced nuts, chocolate fudge, artichoke dip with chips, salmon spread with crackers, and a New York–style cheesecake.

My brother Clifton's family consisted of his wife, Mariam, and his five children. All five children lived in Tallahassee: Justin and his wife, Jennifer; Daniel and his wife; Rachel and her fiancé, Trey; Emily, who was a college student; and, last but not least, three-year-old Anna Grace, a special gift from God from the country of

China. As each of his children's jobs and time allowed, they came to spend as much time with us as they could.

After arriving home from church, we readied ourselves for the excitement of enjoying holiday food, fun and fellowship, and our tradition of exchanging gifts on Christmas Eve. As my nieces and nephews began to arrive, I realized that one of them was just getting over the flu, while another was coming down with symptoms. It entered my mind how detrimental this could be for Bob because of his low blood count as a result of chemo treatments, and for myself, knowing that we had nearly a three-day drive to Houston ahead of us and not knowing how long we would need to be there. Our doctor told us that we should plan to stay a minimum of at least five days. I knew deep in my heart that my nieces and nephews were sacrificing to come, since they didn't feel well and wanted to see us in light of the situation.

As I considered this, I began to pray and ask God to protect us, keep us from getting sick, and for my family to be healed. We continued enjoying the evening, with the exception of the ones who had the flu, as they lay on the couch, forcing themselves to still participate in the gift exchange. We opened presents and celebrated the real reason for the season: Jesus Christ, the Son of God, who was born of a virgin and came down from heaven to earth; Immanuel, "God now with us" (Matthew 1:23). We wanted to capture every moment, to hold on to it, to take it captive to archive in our hearts and minds forever. We finished the evening as usual, very late, with some of us going to bed, while others stayed up having long-overdue conversations.

My niece, who was sick, told us the next day how difficult her twenty-three-mile drive home was. She realized her temperature had been 102 degrees and confessed how difficult the evening had been for her, not realizing she had a fever. She said it alarmed her as she considered how it might affect Bob, hoping and praying that it wouldn't. My other niece, who had spent the night, had experienced symptoms all through the night and had definite signs of the flu.

I was thinking, *Who will be next: my parents, Cliff, Mariam, Anna, or Bob? Will I?* We couldn't! We just couldn't get sick! We had to leave the next day for Houston. My parents were also planning to leave for home to go back to Clarkesville, Georgia. In spite of the circumstances, we continued packing and preparing to head out the next morning, enjoying our last day together.

When we awoke the next morning, my dad stated he felt flu-ish. I was worried but continued to pray, asking the Lord to keep everyone protected and safe, to heal my family, and to be with my parents as they traveled home. I prayed they would make it without incident, as it's certainly not easy to travel when sick.

As I prayed, God reminded me of His faithfulness through scriptures in Lamentations and Isaiah. Lamentations 3:22–24 says, "Through the Lord's mercies we are not consumed, because His compassions fail not. They are new every morning; great is Your faithfulness. 'The Lord is my portion,' says my soul, 'therefore I hope in Him!'" And, Isaiah 26:3–4 promises, "You will keep him in perfect peace, whose mind is stayed on You, because he trusts in You. Trust in the Lord forever, for in Yah, the Lord, is everlasting strength."

The Lord reminded me not to worry, but to trust in Him so that I could have His perfect peace. And I did. I knew in my heart it was going to be okay and that He would take care of Bob and me. We all said our good-byes and hugged, except the ones who had the flu, of course. With them, we bid farewell with heartfelt emotion, but from a distance. It was certainly a time of anxiousness!

The time had finally come to begin our medical trek. Where it would lead and for how long was undetermined. Only God knew.

CHAPTER 8

Houston, Here We Come!

~꧁☙꧂~

The trip to Houston was somewhat exciting, but only as we were able to intermittently put the reality of our situation aside. We were still not showing any signs of getting the flu, and I praised and thanked the Lord as that thought occurred to me.

Since we decided to squeeze in some fun along the way on our trek westward, we stopped at a national historic landmark, the *USS Alabama* battleship on the bay of Mobile, Alabama. At this place, one of America's finest military parks, we experienced a history of heroism spanning from World War II to Desert Storm, more than seven decades. Exploring every floor of the *USS Alabama* took several hours, as the ship was 194 feet tall (taller than a twenty-story building) and 680 feet long. In her day, she had a crew of 2,500 and was called the "Lucky A" because during World War II, there were no American lives lost on board as a result of enemy fire.[16]

It was quite interesting as we worked our way through every room of the ship, trying to put ourselves in the shoes of the servicemen as they actually lived, ate, slept, received medical attention, and served on this great vessel. We finally made our way to the top deck after climbing several stairs and stood at the helm for a while, trying to imagine this great ship in her full glory. The sun was just beginning to set, and it cast its gleaming, almost blinding, golden-pink rays on the horizon. We took in the spectacular view as the day came to a close before us, while also taking a needed rest after our long climb. Thankfully, our exit wasn't the same way, but was an easy ramp back to the park. We decided it was time to get back on track and head westward, find something to eat, and drive a little longer before stopping at a hotel.

Since we were traveling on Interstate 10 all the way to Houston, we also decided to stop in New Orleans. After spending the night in a hotel just hours east of New Orleans, we arrived in the area late morning. We didn't have satellite navigation in our car, so we followed the hustle and bustle and found what looked like the down-town area. We parked and walked around for a while and stumbled upon a happening open-air café that was bustling with excitement. Since a wonderful aroma of freshly baked pastry was drifting through the air, we decided to stroll in and check it out. What we didn't realize was that we had stumbled upon an internationally known café, Café Du Monde. We decided to order what everyone else was ordering—of course, those world-famous sugared beignets along with a café au lait.

Beignets are believed to have derived from the Ursuline nuns of France, who came to Louisiana in 1727. They brought this simple pastry to New Orleans, and the recipe remains the same to this day.[17] The beignets are hand rolled and deep fried, then covered with heaping amounts of powdered sugar and served piping hot.

We were anxious for our order to be taken, so the wait seemed endlessly long. The place was packed, and people were everywhere. I wondered at the time how they could possibly keep up with the crowd. With every passing minute, we debated whether we should leave or not, all the while not wanting to miss this great oppor-tunity to have a famous beignet. We decided to continue waiting a little longer, despite being very hungry since we hadn't eaten lunch.

Our patience was running thin as we reached a forty-five-minute wait and still no one had come to our table. I felt for Bob, since he was getting weary. He had just finished two months of chemotherapy with unpleasant side effects, had lost his hair and beard, and was dealing with facing the unexpected at MD Anderson. We decided to forfeit this long-awaited encounter with the blissful beignet and to walk the streets of New Orleans in search of another restaurant.

After experiencing pure Louisiana culture by trying a muffaletta, we selectively drifted in and out of shops in the French Quarter. Later we stumbled upon another café and decided to get that long-awaited café au lait and rest for a while. After strolling the city streets once more, we heard a wonderful sound springing to life. It was a jazz band tuning up as they readied to play. We followed the sound and nestled into some portable chairs to listen for a while, but we knew we needed to leave soon to get back on the interstate and drive a little farther towards our destination.

We traveled as late as we could, pushing ourselves to make up for the time spent in New Orleans, and finally found a hotel at ten thirty that night just east of Houston. Since we had made better time than planned and were so close to Houston, we decided to sleep in and have a leisurely morning, since our appointment at MD Anderson wasn't until the following day. We purposely wanted to arrive early so we could find our hotel, get settled in, learn the streets, and do a trial run to the cancer center.

After enjoying our morning, we finally arrived in the big city of Houston, Texas, with great amazement and awe. Even though we had grown up in a fairly large city, we had never before experienced the urban sprawl of a big city like Houston. As we continued on the highway, now entering the heart of Houston, I, in a sprightly way, began to hum the theme song to the nightly soap opera *Dallas*. It just seemed appropriate after realizing that we were in the great state of Texas for the very first time, even though it was Houston. The panoramic views as we approached from the interstate were breathtaking! Beautiful architecture was everywhere—certainly an eye-catching view that captured our attention.

We fumbled to find our way to the Holiday Inn Astrodome Hotel at Reliant Park and got lost a few times but did eventually arrive. The large hotel was very quiet, and it appeared that we were the only guests in the hotel that day. It was a very lonely feeling. I wondered if there would be anyone arriving with whom we could share stories, glean information, or befriend. Christmas had just passed, and people were most likely still at home with their families; here we stood, all alone. We had made our hotel reservations well in advance for an undetermined amount of time, and check-in went smoothly.

Because the hotel was in a medical community, it was customary to be given a medical rate, which gives you a superb discount on your daily room rate. But you must be sure to ask for it up front. When you end up staying a few weeks or months, it makes a tremendous difference and is truly a blessing. We settled in on our ninth-floor room, elated that it had a king-sized bed, a picture window that overlooked the city, and all the small amenities to make it feel pleasant. We decided to test our driving directions to the cancer center to ensure a direct route.

After testing our route and feeling confident about the next morning's drive, we decided to seek out what restaurants were in the great state of Texas to experience its true culture. We considered several and finally settled on a down-home barbecue spot. After all, we wanted to experience all that we could of Texas, since we didn't know if we would ever be coming back. The restaurant was unique and the food was great, especially the barbecue. The place was called Goode Co. Texas Barbecue. Months later Bob and I were watching the Food Channel, and that restaurant was featured for their great Texan barbecue. It was neat to see them featured and to be able to say, "Hey, we were there!" So with our stomachs satisfied, we headed back to our room that overlooked Houston's attractive skyline and settled in for the night.

Since our hotel was next to the Astrodome, I was interested in its history and who played there. I discovered the Astrodome's original owner, Judge Roy Hofheinz, had billed it as the Eighth Wonder of the World. It was the first ballpark to have a roof over the playing field. The Astrodome was home to the Houston Oilers (AFL/NFL) from 1968–1997 and the Houston Astros (MLB) from 1965–1999.[18] It sure wasn't hard to tell when something was going on there because we could see the Dome's parking lot. The view of downtown Houston from our room was spectacular, displaying an array of colors as the sun rose and set, reflecting off Houston's broad cityscape.

Chapter 9

Land of the Unknowns

~~◎~~

The next morning was our big day, our first appointment at the famous and internationally known MD Anderson Cancer Center. We arrived with our portable suitcase of records and X-rays and with great anticipation made our way through the maze of buildings, parking lots, and hallways, finally arriving on the ninth floor where the sarcoma center was located. The hospital was so large that it had two Starbucks coffee centers inside. We had certainly never experienced a medical facility like that before!

After being paged, we entered the exam room, and not long after, the oncologist and her nurse came in. We shook hands and were asked to tell our story and provide all our medical records. We also told the doctor we had sought a second opinion on our way from an oncologist in Tallahassee and handed her his report. We explained that he recommended fighting Bob's cancer with all three available methods: chemotherapy, radiation, and surgery. The doctor concluded by saying she would have to meet with the oncology staff to have a multidisciplinary conference to discuss Bob's case. A team of professionals, consisting of a physician, nurse, pathologists, radiologists, pharmacists, dieticians, a case manager, a social worker, and a patient advocate would be available upon request for our every need. We were told that it might take a few days, but they would contact us when ready. So we left the room and made our way through the lobby of this grand place to take in all that the famous hospital had to offer.

We stopped at the Starbucks we had previously passed and treated ourselves to a latte as we explored the various open levels and floors of the complex. We came upon an area that looked like MD Anderson's Hall of Fame, displaying the hospital's medical achievements, technological advances, and cancer-survivor stories. This area was actually called the Visitors Gallery, and it offered inspiration and encouragement to patients, families, and visitors. The story of MD Anderson's history, accomplishments, current activities, and plans for the future was told through the words and images of patients, volunteers, and staff and could also be seen on their virtual e-tour website at www.mdanderson.org. As we exited this area, I couldn't help but wonder where, or if, we would even fall into this slate of medical history and achievements. Would we beat the odds and be featured in the Visitors Gallery as well?

After perusing the area, we decided to head to the main lobby to summon the courtesy shuttle from our hotel. Bob went to make the call as I headed to the nearby lobby. I felt as if I were in another world, walking in a land of unknowns, living a day at a time, walking by faith—faith in our Father God and faith in these doctors. As I pondered what might be the result of our visit, I realized I needed to call our families to inform them of the news of our first consultation.

Finding a seat, I finished updating them and continued to sit in the lobby just staring, gazing at those sitting around me and those walking in and out as they passed through the grand entrance of the hospital. I wondered, as my eyes drifted from stranger to stranger, what they were diagnosed with. What was their story? Were they the patient or the caregiver like me? Was their diagnosis rare like Bob's?

As I drifted in and out from a state of bewilderment to reality, I noticed a highly polished black grand piano in the lobby, so I moved closer. The musician, as well as a flautist, were both tuning up and getting ready to play. They were playing chords of a song I knew well, titled "You Raise Me Up" by the Christian group Selah. It speaks about being down and heavily burdened, but waiting on the Lord even in your loneliness, then how He spiritually lifts you up to go through the storm.[19]

That song had been sung at my church a few months prior, and I never forgot it because it was just after Bob's diagnosis. Even though my heart was heavy, I had a degree of confidence I'd never known. My spirit became determined. I didn't understand it all, but my fear took flight, and I was confident I could go through. I thought, *I'm going to grasp the horns of God's spiritual altar, holding on tightly through the ride, trusting in Him, and allowing Him to raise me up. This is going to be my song throughout this trial!* It would remind me that the Lord was holding me up by His mighty Holy Spirit, knowing that He alone was how we were going to make it through.

I sat there completely spellbound as I listened once again, knowing without a doubt that the Lord was ministering directly to me, a message sent from the throne room of God. As I sat in that lobby, my heart was exploding with joy, elation, and a deep peace that only the Lord and I could measure. I sat there listening and intermittently closing my eyes while tears streamed down my cheeks. Unashamed of them, I continued to fix my eyes on the musicians, focusing on this most precious moment in time. I prayed to the Lord to stall our shuttle so I could finish hearing this heaven-sent music.

Bob and I had attended a jazz concert a few years back, and as the musicians played, I recalled that Bob had closed his eyes while listening to the music. When he finally opened them, he looked at me, smiled, and said, "Try it. You can hear the music better!" So I did, and he was right. You can hear the music better because you are not just listening with your ears, but with your mind and heart.

I had never forgotten that, and while sitting in the lobby that day, I decided to close my eyes so that I could hear the music better, deep within my soul. As the song ended, I looked up, and Bob was sitting beside me, also taking in the moment. But this time was not quite the same as before because his face was laden with a different look, one that was not his usual happy-go-lucky face. At several intervals on our trek, I was painfully reminded of the seriousness of our diagnosis, but I also knew that God was bigger than anything we could ever go through on this earth.

After the song ended—and not a minute too soon— the shuttle arrived, giving us time to gather our things. Psalm 37:4 was on my mind: "Delight yourself also in the Lord, and He shall give you the desires of your heart." As I left that grand lobby, I pondered this precious time the Lord had blessed us with. I knew He had not left us or forsaken us—no, not for one moment! I knew He was confirming that He was still with us and that He cared about *every* detail.

Since it was late afternoon with plenty of daylight left, we decided to take a leisurely drive around Houston to see what we could find. Being in such a culturally rich city and in a nationally known medical community, we didn't have any problem finding something interesting to do. We drove through neighborhoods, observing and comparing the differences in real estate with our home state of Georgia. Older homes in long-established neighborhoods were quickly becoming a thing of the past as they were expeditiously bought and replaced by new mini mansions with zero lot lines. The varied architecture of these newer homes, along with their formal gardens, fountains, iron gates, and striking architecture, was a beautiful sight. Just driving around was enjoyment enough for us on that second day.

While scouting out the area, we also discovered a shopping district called Rice Village. This village is known to most Houstonians as one of the city's oldest and most prized shopping districts. This district exhibits an eclectic personality as a result of its amazing restaurants, antique shops, and boutiques. While driving around, we also saw several other points of interest that we knew we would seek out in the days ahead.

Evening was approaching, so we decided to start looking for a place to eat. We came upon a restaurant called La Madeleine that piqued our interest. It was a French bistro and café, and stepping into this restaurant was like visiting the French countryside; the ambiance was authentic, and the use of fresh food was a priority. From the moment we walked through the door, we felt the harried world disappear as we took in the warm and cozy atmosphere and aroma of enticing French pastries. The relaxing decor included a natural brick interior and a wood-burning fire, warm and glowing. Classical music played softly in the background, enhancing the atmosphere. It bathed us in feelings of comfort and contentment that helped to ease our weary souls. It was a welcome substitute as our lives were turned totally upside down and we were far from home, family, and friends. It turned out to be our most frequented restaurant for breakfast, lunch, and dinner. We did try other cuisines, including Tex-Mex, but this French café won out for at least one meal a day over the following weeks.

The next day we slept in, since we had no definite plans while waiting to hear from the doctor, yet we wondered whether we should get dressed in case they called or fix a pot of coffee, nestle back into bed, and just enjoy our most precious time together. We were in the habit of watching the nighttime hospital series *ER* at home, and it just happened to come on every morning in Houston. So we settled on option two—staying in bed, watching television, and cherishing our time.

The following day we received a call from the doctor's office to come for an appointment around 2:30 p.m. We made our way to her office with great anticipation, but also apprehension, wondering if they had come up with a new approach for Bob's treatment. Much to our dismay, the doctor said that all the doctors concurred that they could not operate because of Bob being in stage 4. This message was all too familiar; we felt so helplessly desperate.

The assessment findings stated that the tumor may have been operable in October, but now, two months later, there were no viable surgical options because a complete removal of the tumor was not likely. Furthermore, the treatment options recommended by Dr. Rost in Tallahassee were not advised because of the tumor's growth. The laboratory findings stated that it was still unclear what type of cancer Bob had, whether it was a C-kit negative gastrointestinal stromal tumor or a smooth-muscle leiomyosarcoma. Without a clear-cut pathology diagnosis, Bob would not be eligible for the C-kit negative Gleevec (imatinib mesylate) clinical trial. More laboratory tests were needed to determine his tumor type and whether he was a candidate for the new, promising chemo drug Gleevec.

The next step was to have MD Anderson's pathologists do advanced lab work on his original biopsy slides taken in October 2003. This would confirm if Bob really did have a negative C-kit result as previously indicated. Bob so desperately wanted that tumor out, and his hopes were dashed with the news that his options were so limited.

Gleevec was not a drug of first choice for LMS, Bob's cancer type, but it was for GIST (gastrointestinal stromal tumors). Gleevec was the first effective treatment for GIST and approved by the FDA in February 2002 for use in metastatic or unresectable (inoperable) GISTs. Gleevec was the first marketed "molecularly targeted therapy" for cancer.[20] This means that the drug only affects specific types of cells, in contrast to conventional cancer chemotherapies that affect all fast-growing cells in the body.

Bob understood that Gleevec could be an option, but he began to emphatically plead, reminding her of what the doctor in Tallahassee had said about treating his cancer with all three approaches. He strongly questioned why their surgical team would not follow Dr. Rost's plan to debulk his tumor by operating. His desperation was evident.

The doctor reiterated what we had been told: because the cancer was growing in the lining of the stomach and had spread to 40 percent of both lobes of the liver, Bob was not a good candidate for surgery. Bob continued to plead his case, progressing into a state of desperation. He said, "Look, I know where this tumor is, and I'll stick a fork in it. Then you'll have to operate." I was utterly astonished, as this was the first time I had seen just how desperate he really was.

The doctor got extremely flustered and continued to discuss the only option she had previously given us but did say that she would talk to the oncology surgeons once again. We did agree to follow the team's recommendation and requested Bob's original biopsy slides. The doctor left, and we anxiously followed as a result of the flurry of emotions. Bob was near tears and shaken, and I'm sure the doctor was ready for us to leave.

It was New Year's Eve, Wednesday, December 31, 2003, and even if we requested the laboratory slides that afternoon, they wouldn't be shipped out until Friday the second, with an arrival date of Monday the fifth. It was already late in the day, and we knew if we didn't call before five, it would add another few days to our wait.

Knowing office staff was sparse because of the holiday added to our volcanic feelings of frustration. The clock was ticking without mercy, so we went to the lobby to gather our emotions and call the lab.

I was frustrated because I didn't understand why I, instead of the doctor, had to make the phone call. What if they asked a medical question I couldn't answer? Because we were so anxious to exit the exam room, I hadn't questioned it. After gaining composure, I called the lab and then family members and friends to give them the latest news, as well as to vent our frustrations.

I was reminded of a scripture in John 12:27–28 when Jesus was about to go to the cross. He said, "Now My soul is troubled, and what shall I say? 'Father, save Me from this hour'? But for this purpose I came to this hour. Father, glorify Your name." In spite of Jesus' suffering, carrying out His Father's will was His only concern. I realized that this too should be my attitude, not just in good times, but also in times of difficulty. Jesus' suffering was certainly nothing that I would ever be called to bear, as He took the sins of the world on Himself, making a way for mankind to be reconciled to God, our creator and father. Knowing this, the least I could do was to relinquish my frustration, let go, let Him work, allow Him to show up, and allow the opportunity for Him to receive the glory. "For our light affliction, which is but for a moment, is working for us a far more exceeding and eternal weight of glory, while we do not look at the things which are seen, but at the things which are not seen. For the things which are seen are temporary, but the things which are not seen are eternal" (2 Corinthians 4:17–18).

We found our journey stalled once again. We were helpless as we waited to get through the holiday season, anxious to get an answer; anxious for the slides to be sent, received, and reviewed; anxious to know if after being tested, the results would come back positive, making

Bob a candidate for Gleevec; and anxious to know what the next step of this arduous journey would be.

This waiting period was costing us. We wanted to get a plan of treatment and return home. The expenses for lodging, meals, laundry, gas, and sightseeing were adding up. I knew my frustration level was nearing its capacity, and I was letting it take me there instead of giving it to the Lord. After all, we were ultimately in His hands anyway; He knew everything we were going through. There was nothing we could do about our situation, so we chose to let go, enjoying our time of not having any plans, going anywhere our senses wanted to take us, and discovering new Texan territory. When we choose to put our trust in the Lord, we can't help but win. When we relinquish our strength, His strength can take over. When our strength fails, His strength begins.

Knowing the city would be in celebration mode, we decided to meander through Houston and see if we could find a way to celebrate the New Year. We had no agenda, but we knew we wanted to celebrate. I knew if we lost our fight with cancer, this would be my last New Year's celebration memory with Bob. But I also knew if we won the fight, we would be reminded of this difficult time during future celebrations.

As we searched, we came upon a place called eatZi's Market & Bakery, and I couldn't hide my delight, urging Bob to pull into the parking lot. Years prior I had worked at a doctor's office, and one of our drug representatives used to bring our office lunch from eatZi's in Atlanta. I recalled the food was delectable, especially their chocolate cheesecake. EatZi's was a very unique European-style gourmet shopping experience. It was a market-style deli, grocery, and café all rolled into one. You could find just about any food in the world there, as well as chef-crafted gourmet items. You could dine in café style or take it out; it was all waiting to be served or carefully packaged for that special, or not so special, occasion.

After perusing the store, we selected a sampling of food and decided to go back to our hotel room to celebrate in a quiet and intimate manner.

We enjoyed the evening, savoring our selections and our special time together, but found ourselves wondering, *Will this be our last New Year's together?* Just as there are many firsts you experience after your loved one passes—first birthday, first Christmas, anniversary, etc.—there is the wonder of firsts in your trial, meaning, is this really the last? As the night neared midnight, we went over to the large picture window in our room to see if there were any fireworks visible on Houston's skyline. I recall Bob said, "I wonder if I will live to see next winter."

Oh, how that question pierced my heart! I solemnly replied, "Oh, honey, how I wish I knew."

The next morning we got a call from a long-forgotten friend, Faye, whom we had worked with years ago while in Fort Lauderdale, Florida. Bob's sister, Cindy, was still in contact with Faye and had been updating her on our situation. Faye just happened to have some Houstonian friends, Charles and Darci, whom she had called while we were there. Charles had also been fighting cancer.

Later that morning we received a phone call from Darci, and she explained they were friends of Faye. She said that on New Year's Day they traditionally chose a stranger to bless, paying it forward. They had decided that we would be their 2004 recipients. They asked if Bob would be interested in getting a second opinion from Charles's oncologist, who had previously worked at MD Anderson. In addition to inviting us for a second medical opinion, they also invited us to come and stay at their ranch. Needless to say, we were astonished at their invitation. We decided to decline, knowing we were probably passing up a once-in-a-lifetime opportunity, but being already settled in at our hotel, we thought it best to stay. We did agree, however, to go to Charles's doctor.

The next morning Charles picked us up at our hotel and drove us to his doctor on the east side of Houston, which is where he and Darci also lived. It was quite a long distance for him to travel. His doctor had worked us in with just one phone call, so I knew we were getting special treatment. When we came to the checkout area, our preferential treatment was confirmed when the receptionist did not ask for our insurance card or hand us a bill. We were astonished that a complete stranger would do this for us. They must have known far too well God's law of sowing and reaping by paying it forward, just like the movie. They were surely exemplifying it!

Unfortunately, Charles's doctor's news was just like all the rest, another dead end. Our hope was disintegrating right before our eyes; another roadblock was dropped in front of us—at least it seemed that way, as far as the medical field was concerned. Charles then drove us back to our hotel, our home away from home. As we rode together, we shared stories, and Charles seemed as if he too could understand our struggle with mortality. It was as though he had pondered the ending we were faced with, wondering how long he too had left on this earth, how much time he had left with his beautiful bride, Darci. After arriving at our hotel, he said that he and Darci would be in touch. The day was an incredible one, being the recipients of such blessing. Bob and I were almost speechless, but we managed to express immeasurable appreciation to Charles.

Because of the holiday, we still had several days of waiting, so we decided to spend the next few days sleeping in, having coffee, watching television in bed, and exploring Houston at our leisure.

I had called our local post office to have our mail forwarded, and it finally arrived. Between all of our business and personal mail, we had quite a stack. As I sorted it into individual piles, separating business mail from family, friends, and bills, I came across a letter from my aunt and uncle. They were so concerned about us, keeping up with our situation through my parents from the beginning. After opening the envelope, I pulled out a long handwritten letter and was surprised when something else fell out. It was a check!

I was shocked as I realized what it was. As I began to read their letter, tears filled my eyes. Because of the lump in my throat, I struggled for the words to tell Bob. They explained they wanted to leave their nieces and nephews money upon their death, but they realized we probably needed it now more than ever. Bob and I were so appreciative and knew once again this was the Lord blessing us through my aunt and uncle. Our medical journey had just begun, and I was already thinking, *How can we ever repay them and others who have blessed us?* Then I thought, *By passing it on!*

I had become familiar with the concept of passing it on years ago after Bob and I had a motorcycle wreck. Many of our friends brought us home-cooked meals, assisted with chores, prayed, and ministered with words of encouragement. I was so overwhelmed with gratitude and asked my friend Gloria, "How can I ever repay all this generosity?"

She had simply responded, "By passing it on!" I never forgot that and still share that story with others. When the movie *Pay It Forward* with Kevin Spacey, Helen Hunt, and Haley Joel Osment came out, I was delighted, as it reminded me what our friends had done.

Saturday afternoon we received a call from Charles and Darci asking if we would like to go to dinner. We had no particular plans that evening, so we said yes. They picked us up at six and insisted on treating us to a fine Houston landmark, Taste of Texas steakhouse. They are known for their Texas hospitality and great service, and they serve aged Certified Angus Beef. After walking through the doors, you feel an air of luxury, yet it feels comfortable.

The restaurant was embellished as fine as the local Texans who graced its tables. The walls and ceilings were adorned with the largest steer horns we had ever seen, and there was Texan decor everywhere. It was truly fine dining Texas-style, and we were once again taken aback by Charles and Darci's extreme generosity.

The next morning I attended a local church service, and after arriving back at our hotel, I picked Bob up to go to a local mall that my brother-in-law, Rich, had told us about. It was considered to be a stellar mall and even had an ice-skating rink inside. The mall was called the Galleria and truly was the finest mall in Houston. In addition to upscale shops like Fendi, Chanel, Gucci, Coach, and Louis Vuitton, it also featured large chains like Foley's and Nordstrom's and was home to about 375 retail stores. The mall was located just west of Loop 610.

To say the least, this mall was a shopper's dream! It was after Christmas, and there were multiple sales we took advantage of, buying gifts for family and friends. One store had a large assortment of unique music boxes and whirligigs, as well as collectibles. They were having a 60-percent-off after-Christmas sale, and our imaginations ran wild as we hand selected various items. Bob was particularly interested in the whirligigs that were suspended from the ceiling. One had a an old-fashioned tin polar bear riding a snow-laden blimp on one end, balanced by oversized sparkling snowflakes on the opposite end; he couldn't resist and bought it.

After finalizing our purchases and enjoying the afternoon shopping, we started looking for a place to eat. While walking through the mall, we came upon the famous restaurant chain the Cheesecake Factory and decided to dine there. After eating, we were too full for dessert but vowed to come back for what made this restaurant famous, their decadent cheesecakes.

Late the next morning, we received a phone call from the oncologist confirming that they had received Bob's slides and would notify us when ready to report their findings. We decided to take off once again but headed south this time to visit the famous city of Galveston, Texas, located on the bay. It was winter, and we had not planned on going to the beach; but Galveston piqued our interest, and we found a boardwalk to stroll called Kemah Boardwalk. It was on Galveston Bay and had lots of unique shops, restaurants, amusements, and a carousel and train, appealing to all ages. We ambled along the weathered boardwalk, checking out the shops and enjoying the freedom from a hurried schedule that was so common at home. We slowly walked arm in arm, the sound of our footsteps echoing from the wooden boardwalk below. The fresh salt air, gently blowing, seemed to carry our worries away.

We soon found an interesting restaurant called Aquarium: An Underwater Dining Adventure. Our adventure began as we were seated around the fifty-thousand-gallon centerpiece aquarium, which allowed exceptional floor-to-ceiling viewing of magnificent sea life as they swam right by our table.[21] With views of this enormous tank, we couldn't help but feel as if we were dining on the ocean floor. It certainly added to our enjoyable boardwalk experience.

After finishing our meal, we strolled the boardwalk once again, taking in the sights, sounds, and aroma of this coastal town, occasionally taking time for Bob to sit and rest. His stamina remained fairly good overall. The sun began to set, projecting rays on the horizon and turning the waterfront into a pink-hued seascape. We decided to conclude our day and found just the right spot to take in the sun's final display of glory.

After the sun disappeared on the horizon, we headed back to Houston, picking up a late snack at Subway before heading to our hotel. While there, we met a lady named Patricia, who was a nurse at MD Anderson. We began conversing, and she inquired, "What brought you here?" We explained Bob's diagnosis, and the more we talked, the more we realized all we had in common: health, nutrition, organics, and our faith. We quickly became friends, and she told us about some nutritionists she wanted us to meet. She offered to pick us up the following morning and drive us to their business, if they were available.

Patricia also asked if we would like to go to Whole Foods grocery store that evening so she could introduce us to some books and health products she thought would help boost Bob's immune system. Bob and I were excited by this encounter and for the help she was offering. We emphatically replied, "Yes, let's go. It's one of our favorite stores!"

Patricia suggested we all ride together, and she would follow us back to our hotel to drop off our car. We insisted on driving, but her persistence prevailed. We were so excited that we wrapped up our half-eaten subs, temporarily suspended our conversation, and got into our car, with Patricia following behind.

During our drive, Bob and I considered how God was orchestrating our every step. Deep down we knew there was a spirit connection with Patricia, and I pondered where this relationship might go. After jumping into Patricia's car, we resumed our conversation, picking up right where we had left off.

After arriving at Whole Foods, Patricia took us to the media aisle to show us some of her favorite books on health. As she began showing us the ones pertinent to our situation, I realized we had purchased some of the same books. Unbeknownst to us, Patricia's nutritionist friends were in the store. Patricia let out a loud gasp as she saw them and shouted out their names. They immediately looked up, and we all sprinted towards one another. Patricia introduced us and explained that we had just met at Subway. We were astonished at how the evening was unfolding, and it was confirmation from God once again.

Patricia asked them, "Are you going to be home tomorrow, and may we come over to see your products?" Considering the situation Bob was in and being quite desperate, we were open to listen to almost any tried product that had testimonials, thinking it might buy him some time. Patricia's friends were agreeable to help and said yes. We stayed at the store chatting a while longer; then Patricia drove us back to our hotel. I could tell the length of the day was beginning to take its toll on Bob, so we welcomed the farewell. We knew that if nothing else came out of our meeting the next day, we would have at least made new friends and learned more about health.

The next morning Patricia picked us up around ten, and we headed out. Upon arriving at her friends' house, we entered their home curious and a little cautious; however, we quickly became comfortable as their warmth and hospitality enveloped us. After a few moments of small talk, we got down to business, discussing Bob's diagnosis.

They excitedly introduced us to their product, Limu Moui, a prized sea plant of Tonga and the South Pacific, and began telling us about its positive testimonies, not just from strangers, but family and friends too. They were distributors of this product and asked if we would like to sample it. Bob and I looked at each other and said, "Sure!" They poured us a shot-sized serving glass, and we gingerly sipped the liquid.

Bob took one look at me, and the next thing I saw was his shot going down the hatch. I, too, finished mine. Since the drink was dark green, we were unsure what it might taste like, but it really wasn't what we had anticipated. It had a grasslike taste, finishing with a bit of a fruity fizz at the end. They also offered us a book by Rita Elkins MH that told all about Limu Moui and its health benefits.

Limu Moui is brown seaweed that is loaded with live plant enzymes that are vital to the human body. When foods are cooked, the live enzymes are actually destroyed. This product has been harvested and consumed by the Tongan people for over three thousand years and displays a wealth of health benefits that have been proven and confirmed by the longevity of the people in their culture. It has a reputation for fighting disease and promoting good health with cancer-fighting abilities. Limu Moui contains a fascinating biochemical called fucoidan, which has been compared to human breast milk for its impressive array of nutrients. Fucoidan has been the subject of several scientific studies, and it is what makes Limu Moui so unique. *Limu* actually means "seaweed."[22]

After drinking this newfound product, Bob decided to purchase a few bottles to take home with us. We enjoyed our time with Patricia and her friends, talking about nutrition and sharing our faith while having a cup of green tea. We ended our morning by joining hands and praying together before heading back to Houston, treasuring just how the Lord had orchestrated our encounter. The morning was certainly one for the journal, and one to be forever filed in the book of our hearts.

It was early afternoon, and we still had a good bit of daylight ahead, so we ventured out again, this time going to Houston's Museum of Natural Science. We couldn't explore the whole museum because of arriving later in the day, but it worked out just fine for the amount of energy we had left. Instead of looking at the glass as half-empty, Bob and I always tried to look at it as half-full. We likened our short day at the museum to a buffet. We didn't have to eat everything; we just enjoyed sampling from the available delicacies we had. So we wandered through the museum, relishing the exhibits that time would allow, seeing the IMAX theater, and viewing the planetarium show.

During the planetarium's show, as the galaxies displayed God's majesty high above me, my mind drifted to why we were in Houston, and I was struck with how minor my problems were compared to others. Seeing the vastness of those galaxies reminded me just how big God is and how small I am.

We wrapped up the day by shopping in the museum's gift shop. It was filled with an array of natural-science items, making our souvenir shopping difficult as we walked from one display to another trying to decide what we wanted to purchase, knowing it would forever remind us of our time here. This well-stocked gift store also reminded us of the wonderful world around us, the world that we so often took for granted, but to which we were now desperately clinging.

We finally selected a collection of multicolored butterflies that had been carefully preserved, named, mounted beneath glass, and set in a striking black shadow-box frame that set off the butterflies' beauty. First Chronicles 29:10–11 says, "Therefore David blessed the Lord before all the assembly; and David said: 'Blessed are You, Lord God of Israel, our Father, forever and ever. Yours, O Lord, is the greatness, the power and the glory, the victory and the majesty; for all that is in heaven and in earth is Yours; Yours is the kingdom, O Lord, and You are exalted as head over all.' "

The following morning we received the long-awaited phone call from MD Anderson's oncology secretary to come for our final consultation. They had a plan of action, and this meant we would be wrapping up our stay and possibly heading home. Our excitement grew as we made our way to the sarcoma center, anticipating good news and the conclusion of our trip.

A multidisciplinary team had concluded that surgery to remove the tumor was not an option. It was recommended that we begin an eight-week trial of Gleevec with monitoring to determine the effectiveness. We had only a small chance that the Gleevec might work, but it was all we had. If after eight weeks of this chemotherapy, there was no response, then palliative chemotherapy of DTIC and Adriamycin would need to be considered. Bob was to have a pretreatment CT scan of the abdomen and pelvis and a PET scan, and repeated scans after eight weeks to evaluate response. He would need close monitoring of his blood counts, liver function, and renal function while receiving Gleevec.

Our hopes were completely dashed as far as having any kind of surgery, but we did have a plan that gave us back some hope. We halfheartedly thanked the doctor for her time and efforts, disappointed that we were going home with less than we had hoped for. We headed back to our hotel and began packing for home.

To celebrate our departure, we decided to go back to the Cheesecake Factory for dinner and to finally indulge in the cheesecake we had promised ourselves. The atmosphere at the Cheesecake Factory had the ambiance of fine dining with soft lighting and music, but it had all the roar of a TGI Fridays with voices reverberating off the walls. The waiters were bustling, the food was plentiful, and the atmosphere electric.

Our final dinner in Houston was one to be remembered as we topped it off with a piping hot cup of coffee and a delectable piece of cheesecake. We each ordered our own slice, knowing we would take half with us to snack on later. Our dinner was enjoyable as we reminisced over the previous weeks, what we had experienced, our first day at the iconic cancer center, the highs and lows of our visit, the cherished moments staying in bed, experiencing Houston's culture and landscape, the people we had met, the Texan fare, and all the great sightseeing we had done. All of it would forever be archived in our hearts and memories.

We were leaving with a plan, which gave us back some hope. With the exception of seeing Dr. Rost, every doctor's visit had made us feel as though we were climbing a dilapidated staircase in an abandoned house, and the steps kept caving in on us. The next morning we checked out of our hotel, leaving the land of the unknowns, and headed back to the great state of Georgia. Oh, how Bob liked Ray Charles's song "Georgia on My Mind"!

CHAPTER 10

Cabin Life—A New Adventure

After returning home with a medical plan, Bob suggested we move into our brand-new rental cabin. Even though we had been renting it for the past four months and reservations were booking fast, it wasn't a difficult decision. We decided the sacrifice of the rental income would be incomparable to what we would gain by making it home. He loved that cabin and said, "I want to experience living there before I leave this world." So we cancelled our rental contract with the management company and moved in at our leisure, leaving our current residence vacant until we figured out what to do with it. We were desperately trying to walk by faith with hope, yet we knew we needed to be realistic and act on the medical information we'd been given. Bob continued to take locksmith calls, but was selective when taking after-hour calls, choosing to cherish and reevaluate his time like never before.

The cabin was just ten miles north of our current home and sat on the riverbank of the Chattahoochee River in the tourist town of Helen, Georgia. The area was surrounded by God's beauty everywhere. From the swiftly flowing river of crystal-clear water that flowed by our cabin, to the ripples that danced as they scurried over the river rocks below our deck, to the varied lush flora surrounding the area, and to the picturesque view of Mount Yonah to the south, living there was like a dream come true. But this dream had the potential to end either with the healing power of Jesus Christ or with the testing of the genuineness of our faith. First Peter 1:6–7 says, "In this you greatly rejoice, though now for a little while, if need be, you have been grieved by various trials, that the genuineness of your faith, being much more precious than gold that perishes, though it is tested by fire, may be found to praise, honor, and glory at the revelation of Jesus Christ." If the latter proved to be true, it would be a not so happy ending for my flesh, but certainly not for my spirit, knowing Bob would be with our Lord.

The story of our cabin began in the spring of the previous year when Bob was called to do a locksmith job for a customer who owned a cabin next to a plot of land. While there, he noticed the lot was for sale. After inquiring about the sale price and finding out we could afford it, his creative wheels started turning. It sat right on the bank of the river, and there was a new water park being built on the opposite side, so Bob saw it as a great investment opportunity. He was always looking for ways to increase our income, and he decided to purchase this lot to have a cabin built with the intention of renting it out as an overnight vacation rental. Living near a resort town and having a few other rental houses, we had a good idea of what type of lodging was most desired by visiting tourists. So we set out to add to our investments by purchasing this select piece of property.

Not long after purchasing the lot, Bob decided to plunge into the challenge of finding house plans that would be conducive to this very small pie-shaped river lot. Being on the river, he knew, would give us the competitive edge that was so needed in the overnight rental market. He labored several months over builders, designs, and log-cabin kits and finally settled on a company that manufactured and built real log cabins in a factory in North Carolina. The exterior walls were made with eight-inch white pine logs, and the interior walls were tongue and groove. The cabin was built in the factory, and after delivery and setup, the second floor and decks were built on site.

After selecting the cabin's design, visiting the model, and ordering it came the arduous task of preparing the foundation for the cabin's eventful delivery. Since the house was going to be built near the riverbank and was in the hundred-year flood plain, a deep foundational base of rock was required by code.

This base of rock was dug twelve feet deep, straight down into the earth, and filled with surge rock. The rock base was finished with an eighteen-inch-thick cement pad on top with strategically placed concrete footers that measured three by four feet. These footers were required to prepare for the nine large pillars that were built on top of them to support the entire weight of the house.

Once the pad was cured and ready, the pillars were formed. They were fashioned into a round steel framework and poured with solid concrete, measuring fourteen feet tall. They not only ensured that the weight of the house would be supported, but also that the cabin would remain above the flood plain, keeping it safe from any rising water.

Next the welders custom welded a twenty-four-inch steel I-beam system on top of the pillars. That was the last and final phase of the foundation process before the cabin would be delivered. The whole methodological system of the building of the cabin was done with precision and integrity.

Just as that foundation was significant to the house's integrity, so is the foundation that we build our lives on. The storms will come, and that is a guarantee. The foundation we have laid will make a difference as to how we weather the storm—how we handle it and how long we can endure.

I had actually started building on the foundation that would hold me up during the years prior to Bob's diagnosis. First Corinthians 3:10–13 says:

> According to the grace of God which was given to me, as a wise master builder I have laid the foundation, and another builds on it. But let each one take heed how he builds on it. For no other foundation can anyone lay than that which is laid, which is Jesus Christ. Now if anyone builds on this foundation with gold, silver, precious stones, wood, hay, straw, each one's work will become clear; for the Day will declare it, because it will be revealed by fire; and the fire will test each one's work, of what sort it is.

It wasn't until Bob's and my motorcycle wreck in August 1990 that I began to rebuild on my foundation that had been laid years prior. The accident was the turning point I so desperately needed, causing me to turn back to the Lord, rededicating my life to Him.

That foundation I added upon had first been laid during infancy when my parents dedicated me to the Lord and was then continued as they took me to church throughout my life. Through those years, that foundation acquired many layers, some firm and some faulty, but ultimately became the rock that would hold me up. Matthew 7:24–27 expresses it well:

> Therefore whoever hears these sayings of Mine, and does them, I will liken him to a wise man who built his house on the rock:

and the rain descended, the floods came,
and the winds blew and beat on that house;
and it did not fall, for it was founded on
the rock.

But everyone who hears these sayings
of Mine, and does not do them, will be like
a foolish man who built his house on the
sand: and the rain descended, the floods
came, and the winds blew and beat on that
house; and it fell. And great was its fall.

In my teen years, I slowly stopped building on that
foundation and started building on another, desiring the
ways of the world because of peer pressure and eventually forsaking the Lord, His love, and His ways, just like
the prodigal son (Luke 15:11–32). I turned from Him
because my flesh was weak as it sought to be accepted
by the world's value system. I believed the lie of the
enemy, the great counterfeiter, Satan.

God, realizing I was not at peace inside but not taking
the leap to restore my relationship with Him, lovingly
and carefully allowed Bob and me to go through our
motorcycle accident. He knew it would get my attention, causing me to cry out to Him once again because I
felt totally helpless and had to depend upon something
greater than myself. He didn't cause the accident, but
He used it.

That's when I also got to witness the depth of Bob's
love and faithfulness to me. Our accident occurred
around 5:45 on a Sunday afternoon. I was more of a
novice than Bob, as far as riding a motorcycle, and after
moving to the country, it didn't take long for him to want
one. His male ego emerged, and he found what he was
looking for—a Kawasaki 750 Vulcan. He wanted his girl's
arms wrapped around his waist, displaying the male
dominance and feminine nature of need that God so pre-
cisely and lovingly created in a man and woman.

We were on a country road that afternoon, going into an S-shaped curve, when an animal ran across our path. Bob tried to dodge it, which caused us to fishtail and lose control. We careened off the pavement for several yards, hitting a five-strand barbed-wire fence head on and causing me to plunge into it head first. Our seat broke in two, but Bob hung on to the motorcycle as it jettisoned down the anterior part of the fence another fifty feet until he was eventually thrown off. He fractured some bones in his leg, and the barbs ferociously clawed his arms and body as he held on for dear life.

After regaining his senses and realizing that I was nowhere around, he frantically started searching for me. He found me unconscious and entangled upside down in the barbed wire. Without hesitation, he put his pain aside and came to my rescue. He untangled the strands of wire from my body, including one that was deeply embedded halfway through my leg, and laid me in the grass. Soon after, I regained consciousness and found Bob leaning over me weeping, thinking I was dead. I felt so helpless and muttered, "It's in God's hands. It's in God's hands."

I couldn't see because my eyes were swollen shut, and I tried to lift my head. When I did, Bob quickly said, "Don't move!" Thinking my neck or back was broken, I relinquished my will to get up and decided to wait for further assistance. Bob was holding my forearm because my wrist had a compound fracture. When I dove into the fence and hit the ground, my hand broke at the wrist, turning it 180 degrees. My body felt like it had been put into a blender and turned on high speed; it was a feeling I had never before experienced.

Even though I didn't know what my future held at that moment, not knowing the extent of my injuries, I had peace, a peace that surpassed any of my understanding and a peace that I knew had to come from the Lord. I turned my thoughts over to Him and waited patiently to be taken care of by the emergency medical technicians (EMTs). I felt secure in the moment and focused on what was directly before me—nothing more.

Bob ran to the edge of the road, desperately looking for help, for any cars that might be passing by. Soon after, a car crested the hill and entered his sight. He frantically waved his arms to get their attention, hoping they would stop. They did and immediately assisted him by finding a cloth to wrap my leg.

Cell phones were not prevalent yet, and since we were on a county road where neighbors were few and far between, finding a phone was a challenge. But God miraculously provided again, because several minutes later, a local EMT was on his way home after working his shift. As he traveled the path that led him home, he was also traveling the path to our assistance, a God-ordained assistance. Just as the ravens came to feed Elijah in a time of drought (1 Kings 17:1–6), God providentially provided for us that day. The off-duty EMT called for an ambulance, and they arrived twenty-five minutes later.

After securing me on the stretcher, they asked if Bob wanted to ride in the front seat or be put on a gurney too. They weren't sure how badly he was hurt, but they did notice he was limping. Since he hadn't taken time to assess himself, putting his pain out of his mind to tend to me, he considered the options. At that very moment, all of his pain and emotions broke loose. His voice cracked, and he said, "My leg does hurt pretty bad, and I think I would like to be checked out too." He was placed on a gurney beside me for our twenty-seven-mile ride to the hospital.

While en route, the EMT radioed our medical statistics to the emergency-room doctor and stated there was "no pulse." When Bob heard that, it quickly got his attention, again causing him to think that I might be dead, but he soon learned they were talking about my hand. There was no pulse in it, and it had been without oxygen for over fifty minutes. It was crucial they get the blood flowing again because the tissue had started to die. Knowing what he had to do, the EMT tried to prepare me and said, "I'm going to have to reposition your hand, and you'll need to be prepared." I mumbled, "Do whatever you need to."

Thirty minutes later we arrived at the hospital, and Bob and I were placed on gurneys before being admitted to triage. Every time they took one of us for X-rays or tests, they made sure we passed each other and said, "Here he [or she] is. We are going to _____. See you later"; and if Bob was close enough, he would reach out and touch me, since I still couldn't see.

Bob was thoroughly checked out and found to have no major injuries except for a fractured leg and superficial lacerations on his arms and body, but he did stay in the hospital overnight for observation. My injuries were a fractured scapula, compound fracture of the wrist, lacerated leg, and exterior lacerations. I needed surgery to have my wrist set and my leg stitched, but I had to wait for an operating room because a major accident had come in that took precedence; in the meantime, they took me into a side room for a plastic surgeon to stitch my forehead and ear. I stayed in the hospital for five days, and my total recovery took about six weeks.

As soon as I was physically able to ride in a car, I went to my friend's church. I hadn't been attending anywhere, and I wanted to rededicate my life to the Lord Jesus Christ as soon as possible. With all my injuries and despite having both arms in slings, I managed to get a dress on, and I hobbled in on one crutch. At the close of the service, I made my way to the altar. I needed to know without a doubt where I would spend eternity. Bob didn't go with me that day, but I felt in time that he would rededicate his life as well.

After the accident, we discussed what each of us had endured: he, thinking I was dead; and I, suffering more injuries. I stated that I would rather receive the injuries than to go through what he did, thinking I was dead. He said, "I still feel like I got off the easiest." He truly proved himself and his love for me that day, and I also knew without a doubt that the Lord had too.

Because I had asked the Lord into my life as a youth, I knew He had not deserted me, but rather, it was I who had deserted Him. Isaiah 12:1–5 says:

> O Lord, I will praise You; though You were angry with me, Your anger is turned away, and You comfort me. Behold, God is my salvation, I will trust and not be afraid; for Yah, the Lord, is my strength and song; He also has become my salvation.
>
> Therefore with joy you will draw water from the wells of salvation.
>
> And in that day you will say: "Praise the Lord, call upon His name; declare His deeds among the peoples, make mention that His name is exalted. Sing to the Lord, for He has done excellent things; this is known in all the earth.

Through the ordeal of the accident and the subsequent rededication of my faith, another layer of my foundation was repaired and built upon once again. Ephesians 2:19–22 says, "Now, therefore, you are no longer strangers and foreigners, but fellow citizens with the saints and members of the household of God, having been built on the foundation of the apostles and prophets, Jesus Christ Himself being the chief cornerstone, in whom the whole building, being fitted together, grows into a holy temple in the Lord, in whom you also are being built together for a dwelling place of God in the Spirit." Praise His holy name—He wasn't finished with me yet!

When building the cabin, we knew fall was a busy season in Helen, so we set a goal for it to be ready to rent out the first week of October 2003. We felt apprehensive as the date approached, fearing that the cabin would not be completed on time. We knew it would be a "first choice" cabin, since people usually asked for a mountain view or to be on a stream or creek, and we quickly selected the name *Gone Fishin'* as its trade name.

The task of customizing the cabin to meet overnight vacationers' desires was a fun challenge for us, and we were passionate about preparing for it. Bob labored many nights to carefully plan every detail of the cabin's construction, being careful to maximize the river views from every room. I was going to Bible college at the time, and upon my returning home, we would often stay up late fine-tuning the plans that he had worked on while I was away. He carefully considered the size of each room, penciling in probable furniture with scaled miniature models to get the right perspective. After several months of laboring over specifications, phone calls, and visits to the factory to inspect the construction progress, the cabin was finally completed and ready to be delivered.

The day of delivery was exciting as the cabin came in two separate sections, each on its own eighteen-wheeler flatbed truck. Each section had to be carefully set onto the steel foundation by a large crane. Once this was done, the actual build-out process of the second floor, stairs, and surrounding decks was begun, taking another four months to complete on site.

As the cabin neared completion and our target deadline to rent it approached, we began the frenzy of shopping to furnish it. We visited antique malls and specialty stores to collect wild animals and fishing memorabilia, stockpiling just the right items to furnish the cabin with a fishing theme.

The back deck projected high above the river to give a panoramic view, and it made you feel as if you were in your own private treehouse. The river approached the cabin and continued descending past it, eastward, downstream, as if on its own unforgiving mission toward the Gulf. It was a sight to behold. The view of the river left you feeling pure contentment and peace, but also inspired feelings of great respect, feelings that would be proven valid several times over the next few years.

Just prior to completion, we listed the cabin with a local rental-management company to begin accepting online reservations. Their website offered a virtual tour and online booking, so it didn't take long for reservations to start coming in. Once guests got a taste of the Gone Fishin' experience, the cabin's guest book began to fill up with personal stories.

Two weeks after contracting with the rental company, Bob received his devastating diagnosis. He thought about moving into the cabin but decided to consider it further. After returning from MD Anderson, he didn't think twice—he wanted to live there. Choosing to cancel our rental contract was bittersweet—sweet for us, but bitter for the guests who wanted to return.

After receiving his diagnosis, Bob was eager to start the oral chemo drug Gleevec, yet we knew our chances for a positive response were slim. We scheduled an evaluation with Bob's oncologist in Gainesville, Georgia, for a post–MD Anderson appointment, as suggested.

He concurred with MD Anderson's findings and suggested we get started with Gleevec right away. He wrote the prescription for Bob and explained we would need to be prepared to pay for it because it would be several thousand dollars. Because we were self-employed, our medical insurance plan required us to pay for our prescriptions first, then turn them in for a refund. After calling our pharmacist, we were told that the first round of Gleevec would be $3,620.95. Fortunately, we were able to put it on our charge card and then file for reimbursement.

Before starting Gleevec, we scheduled CT and PET scans as suggested by MD Anderson. For comparison purposes, these scans were to be repeated when the second round of Gleevec was completed. We also scheduled several doctor's visits to closely monitor Bob's blood counts, liver function, and renal function while receiving the drug.

After taking Gleevec for a few weeks, Bob remained fierce in spirit. He was fueled by hope and purpose and was resolved to get through the chemo and move into the cabin. Bob was concerned about taking care of me and wanted to sell his business in preparation for the worst. Proverbs 13:12 says, "Hope deferred makes the heart sick, but desire fulfilled is a tree of life" (NASB). Hope can certainly bring life, and that it did!

The idea of downsizing from our 2300-square-foot home of ten years to a 1500-square-foot cabin was challenging at first. The cabin was fully furnished, right down to everyday cooking utensils and linens, which meant we needed to limit what we brought to just personal items and things that made it feel like home. I knew we would eventually have to consider what to do with our primary residence, but that could come later. For being a vacation rental, the bedroom closets were spacious, but the cabin lacked the storage necessary for full-time living. We brought what we could to make it comfortable and left the rest in our house to be decided upon later.

Eventually we tossed around the idea of having an estate/garage sale. It broke my heart to think that we would be selling most of our possessions, but ultimately I knew that nothing we owned really belonged to us anyway. Bob and I were just borrowing it while we were on this earth. Matthew 6:19–21 says, "Do not lay up for yourselves treasures on earth, where moth and rust destroy and where thieves break in and steal; but lay up for yourselves treasures in heaven, where neither moth nor rust destroys and where thieves do not break in and steal. For where your treasure is, there your heart will be also." While our flesh struggled with leaving things behind, our spirits knew nothing could steal the memories that were sealed in our hearts and minds.

In the midst of dying to my flesh through the loss of our possessions, I was also reminded that I am a steward. The Bible says we are stewards over the earth (Genesis 1:26), stewards of the Lord's unearned grace (1 Peter 4:10 and Ephesians 3:2), and stewards over our relationship with the Lord God and His gospel through His Son Jesus Christ (1 Corinthians 9:14–18). These scriptures gave me a whole new perspective on the responsibility I had as a Christian and the free gift I had received of His mercy and grace. I recognized the truth in the biblical concepts of stewardship and building my treasure in heaven, and I knew it wasn't important what we kept or gave away.

Still, my heart was breaking in thinking about selling our belongings. I knew if Bob were to die, I would most likely have regrets about what we sold, since I wouldn't have these things to remind me of him. (I did, however, decide to keep some of our most treasured items.) The Lord quickly reminded me that the memories written in the book of my heart were there forever, to recall at my choosing. So when Bob suggested we move to the cabin, instead of focusing on the possible heartache that could come from it, I thought, *I'm going to look at this as a chance to live out Bob's life and create new memories together, even if they are bittersweet.*

We finally got settled into our new abode and began to enjoy the new season of our life while Bob continued to take his oral chemo. He suffered with bouts of nausea, but it was manageable. He still worked on the days that he felt up to it, all the while pushing to sell his business.

He had been wooing a young man who was toying with the idea of buying our business but wasn't quite ready to make the commitment. He was riding with Bob on service calls, as his job would allow. He knew buying our business was a good opportunity, but he wanted to see how difficult it would be to learn the locksmith trade first. After a few months of riding with Bob, learning the trade, and many words of encouragement, he finally decided to take the leap of faith and buy our business in February 2004.

The day that the deal was finalized felt like sending our child off to college; we were filled with exhilaration, yet at the same time, great sadness. We knew that all of the energy we had put into our business was being entrusted to someone else. Bob had started his business almost eleven years earlier, diligently working to make it grow. The fact that his business sold proved it had become something of value. He was so glad the deal was finally complete and that his business would continue without him. He had worked so hard and was so proud when it sold. What a day of celebration! Bob jingled the keys while handing them over to the new owner, Cranley, danced his famous jig while beaming, and said, "It's yours now, and I get to be the passenger!"

Even though Bob's actions were jovial, his heart felt like it was on a chopping block. He continued to train and ride with Cranley every chance he felt up to it. With the burden of selling his business off his shoulders, he could concentrate on his medical needs and also do a little traveling.

One winter day, snow had fallen, gently covering the ground with a fluffy glistening powder. It was somewhat dreary out, yet beautiful in its own solemn way. Bob and I walked out onto our covered back deck to survey the beauty and noticed how the snow was kept at bay by the flowing water's edge. The river stood out cold and a dreary dark gray as it was contrasted against the bright white snow. I remember thinking as I put my arm around Bob's waist, *Will this be the last winter we will ever see together, or will there be another?* Oh, how blessed I felt to be able to stand there with him, witnessing this unspoken beauty with my eyes, yet my heart was sad.

Bob finished his two rounds of Gleevec and was finally due for his postscans to see if it had been effective. He never missed an opportunity to whirl off a joke, even when he wasn't feeling great. While getting his PET scan, he relayed a joke to the technician about a lady who needed an X-ray to find out what was wrong with her.

He explained, "The technician laid her on a table and proceeded to bring a dog into the room. Securely holding the dog's body, he moved it all around her, back and forth, slowing scanning the sides of the woman's body.

"The puzzled woman quickly said to the technician, 'What the heck are you doing?'

"The technician replied, 'You wanted a PET scan, didn't you?' " Our technician looked at Bob, then me, and shook her head.

Building the rock base for the cabin in Helen, Georgia, 2003

Crane setting up first half of log cabin

Crane setting up second half of log cabin

Cabin build-out on site

Gone Fishin' cabin completion, September, 2003

CHAPTER 11

A Perilous March, but to Victory?

T he results of Bob's scan were disheartening; the Gleevec had rendered no effect on his cancer. The report showed that the stomach tumor had continued to grow, and there were more spots on the liver than before. There was no other option other than palliative chemo, which is given to patients for relief only, not as a cure. Our news had worsened, but our determination and will to press on did not waver. In spite of our circumstance, we chose to walk by faith, faith that the Lord was working all things out for His glory. After all, we had determined that we would win in life or in death.

When Lazarus's sisters called for Jesus to come heal their brother, Jesus said, "This sickness is not unto death, but for the glory of God, that the Son of God may be glorified through it" (John 11:4). I knew in my heart that Bob's sickness was not unto death. Even if his body were to die, his spirit would live forever with the Lord. This trial of sickness could reveal the power, presence, and peace of God, bringing glory to His name.

As we waited to start palliative chemo, we decided to take some things from my flower garden and donate them to the church garden I was starting. This garden was not your normal flower garden; this was a kingdom-teaching garden. It was specifically created to teach God's Word based on Romans 1:20, to show that everything in nature reveals God's invisible attributes, eternal power, and godhead so that man has no excuse not to know Him. I had been writing curriculum to teach about the garden during Sunday school and vacation Bible school and was anxious for the garden to be established so I could start teaching from it.

God had given me plans for this garden on a grand scale, but for the time being, I had to go with an alternative plan, knowing I did not have the time I needed to invest in it. The plan was to have a rectangular-shaped garden with a grapevine growing in the middle. He is the vine—the life—and we are the branches. Apart from Him, we can do nothing and will eventually die. The grapevine was to be accessible from all sides and represented that God is accessible at all times.

The four surrounding quadrants were to consist of a butterfly garden, praise garden, prayer garden, and a fruit garden, each representing unique attributes of God and His gifts given to us. These gardens were to have paths, benches, arbors, raised beds, birdhouses, a birdbath, and specific trees, shrubs, flowers, and fruiting landscape to represent God's kingdom. The entire garden would reveal spiritual truths in the physical realm, telling His story through nature. It would allow His believers, not only to get to know Him, but also to be able to spend time with Him. The church body could also use it as a place to have lunch, rest, and refresh.

The less elaborate, alternative kingdom-teaching garden I created faced the east where the sun comes up, and it consisted of five raised beds, each in the shape of the sun's rays as it dawns on the horizon. The beds were eight feet long, four feet wide at the top end, and three feet wide at the bottom end, thus emulating the rays of the sun.

This layout was inspired from the wilderness tabernacle God directed Moses to build. Whenever it was set up, God directed the opening to face the east. While reading Malachi 4:2, it occurred to me the reason why: because the sun comes up in the east—light. Jesus is the light! Light dispels the darkness. The sun also rises, which symbolizes resurrection life. Jesus is resurrection life that gives light to all men. Even though Jesus wasn't living at that time, He was being revealed through an Old Testament teaching.

One particular day upon initial setup of the garden, Bob and I were delivering a decorative metal-arched trellis and a cement birdbath with an angel centerpiece. As we approached the back of the church property, we had to stop to open a very large iron gate that swung long and wide. The sky was blue and the day was bright with sunlight as we delivered them. Just as we were finishing our task, a heavy rain shower began to fall. We raced to complete the last detail and quickly jumped into our truck.

As we drove across the back lot to exit, I realized I was going to have to get out and open the iron gate again. By then it was raining quite hard. I thought, *Oh no, I'm going to get soaked!* As we approached the gate, it began to slowly swing open towards us, as if purposely inviting us to drive through it. With amazement I shouted, "Did you see that? That has to be the Lord! There is no wind anywhere!"

As we drove through the gate, Bob came to a complete stop so I could jump out to close it, and just as he did, there was a rainbow in full view right in front of our truck. I knew without a doubt that the Lord was confirming His presence, not just to me, but especially and purposely to Bob. He was revealing Himself in the only way that He does—in a totally personal way. There was no doubt in my mind that the Lord was saying, "This sign is for you. I'm here! Don't fear, my child." Just as

He confirmed His covenant promise to Noah by setting a bow in the sky, He was confirming His promise to us—"I will never leave you or forsake you."

A few weeks after that happened, I was reading my Bible, and God took me to Acts 12. It explained how an angel came to Peter while he was in prison and helped him escape. It said that the iron gate of the prison swung open of its own accord. As I read it, I chuckled and said to God, "You brought me to this scripture to remind me that You showed up, that You are here. Wow! Thank You! I love You, Lord."

Since palliative chemo was the next and only step of Bob's medical journey, we decided to trade in our 1999 Town and Country van for a new and fully loaded 2003 model. Knowing we were free to travel because there were no more medical options, we didn't think twice about purchasing this new vehicle because we wanted to use the time Bob had left to travel. With our business sold, we simply focused on having no agenda other than enjoying each day as a precious gift.

With a brand-new van in our possession and an eagerness to test it out, I called Bob's sister, Cindy, to see if she wanted to take a mini trip with us to Savannah, Georgia, for a long weekend. Knowing Bob's diagnosis, Cindy wanted to take some vacation time to spend with him. She jumped at the chance, scheduled her flight from Fort Lauderdale, Florida, and flew up.

Bob and I had been to Savannah many times, but never in the spring, and the city was bursting with color. As we entered one of Savannah's many squares, the pink and white azaleas blooming everywhere were a head-turning feast for our eyes.

Our days were spent walking the historic River Street district, strolling in and out of shops, tasting samples of mouth-watering pralines, and taking in the sights and sounds of the river walk's local entertainers. A pair of street performers we focused on was a father-and-daughter team. The father had adorned himself from head to toe in a homemade musical ensemble. It was made with musical instruments of every sort, each meticulously connected to his hands and feet. This one-of-a-kind, all-inclusive instrumental band was crafted so he could play solo wherever he went. As every inch of his body moved to give life to this one-man musical machine, his tall, lanky eleven-year-old daughter danced unabashedly beside him, welcoming dollars from the audience. She danced with abandon, as if she had no cares in the world. We all sat spellbound, watching intently as they performed. They brought pure joy to us in that moment.

Later that day we decided to eat at Paula Deen's restaurant, the Lady & Sons. We had eaten at this famous Savannah restaurant the year before, and our mouths watered as we anxiously waited to feast on the wonderful Southern fare.

As evening approached, we decided to finish our day by hailing a red-and-white-striped pedicab. Bob, Cindy, and I crammed into the canvas-cradled backseat while the pedicab driver, a young college-aged man, convinced us that, despite our collective weight, he could peddle us through the historic Savannah streets. We could barely stop laughing as we pondered how this young man could peddle with us crammed in behind him, trying not to crush one another. After emphatically assuring us that he could manage it, he began his assent, pointing out historical and noteworthy points of interest along the way. I couldn't help but think, *What a great evening, one that will certainly be recorded in the pages of our memory book!*

Bob continued to press on with a tenacity that I had seen many times before. It always amazed me that he never focused on any unfortunate part of a situation, let alone the major trial he was experiencing. He was so happy to be alive and focused on making the most of his experiences. He always said, "I feel so blessed!" He wanted to be around a little longer to be able to tell his story, to share what he had learned about life, love, and the pursuit of it all. He wanted to tell anyone willing to listen so that they too might learn to live with joy and hope, even in the face of adversity.

It was April 14, Bob's fifty-first birthday, and since his sister was still in town, we decided to celebrate. Bob felt good, so he rode with Cranley that day, continuing to impart technical wisdom. Upon his return home, the spring weather beckoned for an outdoor gathering, so we celebrated Bob's birthday by having birthday cake and ice cream on our back deck. Even though Bob was playing the waiting game, he had a little bounce back in his step. He was still on a mission until he took his last breath, a mission of joyfully sharing his wisdom with the world.

To get Bob ready for the upcoming treatments of palliative chemotherapy, Bob's doctor had decided it was time to have a port installed, also known as a portacath, atrial catheter, or central line. A port is a small device that is implanted and sutured just under the skin in the chest area. It is usually used for the delivery of ongoing treatment to eliminate the discomfort of numerous needle sticks. It allows the infused treatment to spread through the body very quickly by going directly into the bloodstream through a large vein that leads to the heart, ending in the right atrial chamber. At the base of the port is a narrow, flexible tube called a catheter, which is inserted into the vein during a brief surgical procedure performed under local anesthesia.[23]

The port is about the size of a half dollar, with a slightly raised rubber area. Because this rubber area self-seals when it is punctured, it allows the port to be punctured several hundred times with greater ease and less discomfort to the patient. A port also serves to eliminate the possibility of the drug coming into contact with the skin, which could cause possible side effects. The port is used not only for administering treatments, but also for drawing blood. Every time Bob needed any blood for lab work, he was delighted that he didn't have to have a needle stick in his arm. After implantation of the port, he was given a port identification card, which was to be kept with him at all times and given to every medical professional who treated him.

The surgical oncologist that originally diagnosed Bob was the one who performed this procedure. After looking at Bob's reports, the doctor couldn't believe he was doing as well as he was. He said, "By the looks of your liver scan, I can't believe you are not flat on your back." Even though the reports showed death's march toward destruction, Bob's stamina, attitude, and demeanor were still victorious. Praise the Lord, He was confounding the wise! As 1 Corinthians 1:27–29 says, "But God has chosen the foolish things of the world to put to shame the wise, and God has chosen the weak things of the world to put to shame the things which are mighty; and the base things of the world and the things which are despised God has chosen, and the things which are not, to bring to nothing the things that are, that no flesh should glory in His presence."

A visit to the oncologist before starting palliative chemo also confirmed that Bob's date with death had been stalled. After reviewing the scans that were taken, the doctor said, "I've got some good news. Your stomach tumor is growing out into the body cavity instead of inward towards your other organs." We were sad at first, but then elated when we realized it was a blessing. This gave us hope that time was on our side. Even though the tumor was still there, it was defying the odds. We could again see God's hand at work in our situation.

Not only was the Lord showing up, but we also felt Bob was doing so well because he was taking heavy doses of a glyconutrient product called Ambrotose®.[24] This product had numerous positive testimonials. After

Bob was first diagnosed, my mom began telling her friends of his prognosis, and one friend suggested he start on this nutrient right away. Because of the scientific and media validation that glyconutritionals were getting, and because the product was listed in the 2002 Physician's Desk Reference (PDR), we were confident that Bob should take these supplements.[25]

The recommended dose for a healthy adult was one-quarter teaspoon two times a day, but since Bob was considered "severely medically challenged" under the company's guidelines, he was to take four tablespoons a day. This was quite a task for him as well as a financial burden, but when you are fighting for your life, your priorities change very quickly.

Ambrotose® came in the form of a fine white powder that was practically tasteless and could be mixed in water or juice. There were other products the company sold that Bob also took: Ambrotose AO™, an anti-oxidant cell-protection formula with immune support; Glycentials™, a multivitamin; Phyt-Aloe®, a powder of dried fruits and vegetables; Plus, which supported optimal endocrine health; and MannaCleanse™, an intestinal health-support product with added beneficial flora. This regimen was a lot to endure at first, but Bob was up for the challenge. As time forged on, these products, along with prayer, proved to be integral in prolonging Bob's life expectancy.

The story of Ambrotose actually begins with aloe vera. In the late 1980s, Dr. Bill McAnalley, a research pharmacologist, was determined to identify the active component in aloe vera. After many years, he discovered the functional component in aloe vera that is responsible for its health-promoting properties. To his surprise, the active ingredient was a carbohydrate with many mannose sugar molecules linked together. He found that aloe products are not effective unless the active carbohydrate molecule has been stabilized, and he developed a special patented process to maintain that effectiveness. Today the pharmaceutical and dietary supplement versions of this standardized aloe substance are protected by over 100 patents in numerous countries. The dietary supplement was named Manapol®.

The positive feedback from the extensive use of Manapol overwhelmingly demonstrated that it supports the immune system. It was also clear that many of the results were not limited to immune support, as there were numerous reports of improved cognitive (mental) function. This puzzled Dr. McAnalley, who by then was a leading scientist in the little-known field of carbohydrate research, and he decided to investigate further.

The journal *Biotechnology* (February 1990) stated that almost without exception, whenever two or more living cells interact in a specific way, cell-surface carbohydrates, or simple sugars (not table sugar!), are involved. These cell-surface carbohydrates act as codes, telling every other cell who they are, what they do, and whether or not they are healthy. This code system is so basic to human life that it is the means by which a sperm recognizes an egg for the purpose of fertilization.

The 1996 edition of *Harper's Biochemistry* (chapter on glycoproteins by Dr. Robert K. Murray) identifies eight essential carbohydrates necessary for cell-to-cell communication. When Dr. McAnalley saw that mannose, the carbohydrate in Manapol, was listed as one of those eight essential carbohydrates, it all started to make sense. He realized that glycoproteins were essential for the body's genetic code and could have a crucial role in the maintenance of optimal health.

Since only two of the eight carbohydrates identified in *Harper's Biochemistry* are found in adequate quantities in our modern diets, Dr. McAnalley decided to find good plant sources of all essential carbohydrates associated with cell-to-cell communication (including Manapol) and combine them in a dietary supplement. The result was glyconutritionals, and Dr. McAnalley called his new product Ambrotose, because the Greek word *ambrosia* means "nectar of the immortals." He added the suffix because in chemistry a substance that is a sugar ends in *ose*.

In 1997, *Science and Medicine* reported that five of these essential carbohydrates had been found in human breast milk. In 1998, a respected scientific journal, *Acta Anatomica*, published a special edition on glycosciences.[26]

Bob started the first round of palliative chemotherapy with DTIC and Adriamycin, commonly known as "red devil." It was called red devil, not only because it was red, but because it was brutal on the body. The doctor said the treatment would lower Bob's blood count and most likely require blood transfusions. Bob would need periodic echocardiograms to make sure his heart was not being damaged by this aggressive chemo.

These treatments were administered through a pump that was fastened around Bob's waist and worn home for continual infusion over a seventy-two-hour period. The pump infused this red chemo through a clear tube that flowed directly into Bob's heart through his port. The red color and its results confirmed the name red devil!

Even though it zapped Bob's health and stamina, his lab work always managed to pass the requirements for continued treatment without a transfusion or hospitalization. I believe prayer, the aloe product, and the nutritional supplements helped him stay within the allowable limits. Overall, he was given the maximum allowable dose of eight infusions, which were administered from April to October 2004.

When he went for his second round, as the nurse was installing the unit, Bob said, "I'm getting a hemi today."

With a puzzled look, she repeated with her strong Asian accent, "Hemi— what is dat?"

Bob said, "You know, *hemi* for *hemorrhoid*, because wearing this is a pain in the butt."

She busted out laughing, which became instantly contagious, and the whole chemo room began to laugh. All the nurses looked at Bob, grinned, and shook their heads.

Not long into the treatments, Bob began to decline. He slept for days, often eating nothing. I would concoct nourishing milk shakes and drinks that were loaded with nutrients and quite palatable, but he would take one sip and turn back over in bed. It broke my heart because not eating accelerated his decline. I would turn to go back to the kitchen with tears in my eyes and a heavy heart.

Before starting round three, Bob's lab work and white-blood-cell count came back "marginal." He continued to lose weight, and his coloring was often sallow. Because of the loss of his facial hair, I began to notice people staring at him. It made me more determined to show my love for him when we were in public, and I would put my arm in his, pressing closely as if to say, "I know you don't know our story; that's why you're staring. But this is my beloved husband, for better or for worse, in sickness and in health." I wanted to send a statement to them—that I loved Bob unconditionally, "till death do us part," and that I was proud to be his wife in spite of our situation.

Bob learned to love the Food Network channel. When he had stamina to sit up, he watched it into the evening while sitting in his favorite chair. It was a godsend because it whet his appetite. We especially enjoyed Rachael Ray's show *$40 a Day*. She visited different towns, exploring the best food on her budget of forty dollars for three meals a day. This inspired us to take some short day trips to experience the places she had visited, one of which was Rembrandt's Coffee House in the Bluff View Art District of Chattanooga, Tennessee.

We loved coffee, and the coffee house was only three hours away. It was a delightful trip and especially neat to stand where Rachael Ray had ordered her decadent miniature chocolate-coffee-cappuccino cup filled with a sinfully delicious filling. Rachael became our friend as she entered our home and lives every night through her show. We watched eagerly as we waited to see where she would travel next. After realizing how much the Food Network influenced his eating, Bob told his oncologist that he should recommend watching the Food Network to all of his chemo patients.

Since we were going on day trips as his strength allowed, Bob wanted to search for a new Volkswagen convertible. We were traveling quite a bit, so we thought it would be good to have a fun car to travel in. Bob didn't have the strength to physically shop for a car, so he decided to shop online. After many phone calls, he finally found a car for the right price with all of his desired features, and the dealer even promised to deliver it to our cabin. It was a turbocharged, cyber-green Volkswagen with creamy-colored leather seats and a black convertible top. The black top contrasted with the cyber green and gave it a striking look. Since it had a premier sound system, we were anxious to take it for a spin.

Our first trip—with the top down, of course—was to the picturesque town of Highlands, North Carolina. Lowering the top was easy; with the quick release tab and the push of a button, the top neatly tucked away and you were exposed to nature in seconds. We loaded up some gear, stopped at the first coffee house to get a latte to go, and headed out. Bob felt well enough to enjoy the ride, but shortly after arrival, he was ready to return home.

Bob's appetite was poor, and I learned early on to be patient with him. I tried not to push him when he didn't want to eat, but would encourage him to do so to keep up his strength. I later learned that his stomach tumor was taking most of the nutrition from any food that he ate. It made me angry, and I thought of the tumor as a monster, as did he.

In retrospect, I wondered how well Bob really was coping, especially because of the jaw-dropping statement he first made to the oncologist at MD Anderson when he said he would "stick a fork in it." Since he never complained, one day I asked if he would share how he felt. He responded by saying, "It's not worth complaining, Kim. Life is too short!" Knowing his sweet spirit and personality, I knew to accept his reply and not dig further. I felt his pain even though he never discussed it. I believe he knew I was suffering with him, but silence was his way of dealing with it, and I had to respect that.

It broke my heart, and sometimes when we lay in bed, I would have to turn over so he couldn't see the tears falling down my face. At times I felt like my heart might burst. I wanted to sob but needed to hold it in so he wouldn't hear me. I knew I needed to be strong for him. I couldn't go into another room for privacy because our cabin was so small. There were times when I was alone and was able to let my emotions flow, although my pain was never fully alleviated when I did. I knew, however, of the challenge that was still before us, and I was determined to press forward.

By the time Bob finished round three of chemo, his tumor had caused him to appear about six months pregnant. He was due for a PET scan to see what chemo was accomplishing besides a decline in his quality of life. He said, "I'm tired of being sick!" One day after several people had called to ask how he was doing, he asked my mom, "What are you supposed to say when people ask how you feel, when you are dying?" He didn't say it, but I think he wondered if they really believed his prognosis. Maybe they were in denial.

I think they understood but just didn't know how to deal with it. One of his closest friends avoided him and interacted only on occasion. I began to see the need for educating others on dealing with terminal illness and death and was determined to do something about it;

I saw a need to help others understand. We will all, at some point or another, have to deal with trials, illnesses, and death and will need to know what to say or how to handle it. I know it's not easy to communicate when someone is dealing with a rare disease or a terminal prognosis, but it's valuable to learn how. Relationships can be fragile, even in normal situations, but we must learn to navigate the complexities of relating to a person who is suffering or facing death. I was determined to educate people so they could be prepared to respond rather than react.

One day while talking to a friend about this, she asked, "Then what do you say to someone who is facing death?" I told her to let the patient steer the conversation. Start by telling them you have been thinking of them or praying for them. Ask if there is anything you can do for them or help them with. Ask and wait for their response, and then follow their lead.

Specifically, do not ask, "How do you feel?" That is a direct question, and a patient who is in denial may not want to answer you that day. They may divert the conversation. If they do, be a good listener and talk about whatever they bring up. Another question you might ask is, "Would you like me to pray specifically for anything today?" If it's appropriate, pray with them. If you do not feel comfortable praying, then give them a hug and tell them you will pray for them.

There are five emotions a patient, family member, friend, or caregiver can go through when dealing with illness, grief, or loss: denial, anger, bargaining, depression, and acceptance.[27] There is no order in which these emotions must occur, and you may experience certain ones multiple times throughout your journey. Knowing these emotions and what someone may be experiencing can help you understand their behavior. I don't recall Bob outwardly experiencing any of them, other than denial, but I suppose he may have privately.

Overall, he continued to make the most of every moment, often throwing you a fast-pitch one-liner to make you laugh. Once when he was in intensive care, the nurse told him he was getting a steak-and-potato dinner in his intravenous line. Later that evening, his IV alarm went off because of a crimped line, and his nurse quickly entered the room to address the problem. While she was leaning over his bed, Bob said, "Oops! A potato must have gotten stuck in the line!" Even in his miserable state, just one day after life-threatening surgery, he still managed to have a sense of humor.

Upon learning about this grief process, I decided to gird my mind, set myself like flint, and stand on the Rock that was holding me up. I had not denied Bob's diagnosis. I had not gotten angry with God. I wasn't going to bargain with God about it or be depressed—sad, yes, but not depressed. I believed that because I was a strong Christian woman, I had not experienced any of these emotions.

While I felt that I did not experience this process, there is nothing wrong with feeling any of these emotions. In fact, God showed me it was okay to express them and to question Him if I needed to. Psalm 50:15 says, "Call upon Me in the day of trouble; I will deliver you, and you shall glorify Me." Psalm 71:20–21 states, "You, who have shown me great and severe troubles, shall revive me again, and bring me up again from the depths of the earth. You shall increase my greatness, and comfort me on every side." How wonderful to know that I have a Father who is always waiting to act on my behalf, whose heart yearns for me to need Him so that He can rescue me and comfort me. Why wouldn't He? He created me! He knows me and my every thought.

God knows my thoughts before I even speak them. Psalm 139:4 declares, "For there is not a word on my tongue, but behold, O Lord, You know it altogether." Psalm 40:5 proclaims, "Many, O Lord my God, are

Your wonderful works which You have done; and Your thoughts toward us cannot be recounted to You in order; if I would declare and speak of them, they are more than can be numbered." His thoughts of me, Bob, or anyone cannot be counted. What an incredible thought!

The results of the PET scan after the third round of chemo were back, and we were scheduled to see the doctor to discuss the results. Much to our surprise, the doctor entered the room and said, "I have good news! There are no new cancer cells." Bob's cancer was being suppressed, which meant the chemo was stopping the tumor cells from multiplying but not diminishing the stomach tumor or liver cancer. Even though this was small in the scheme of things, it gave us great encouragement, knowing that it might give us more time, for only God knows the day and hour of our end.

Our spirits were renewed, and we decided to take a trip to Saint Augustine to celebrate with Bob's sister, Cindy, her husband, Rich, and their ten-year-old daughter, Emily. After enjoying the weekend with them, we started planning our next trip on a chartered bus tour of Niagara Falls, the Hershey factory in Pennsylvania, and Pennsylvania Amish country. Bob was due to start round four of chemo but thought he could make the weeklong trip before starting.

Everything on the trip was planned, so we didn't have to do a thing except write a check, pack our bags, and show up. Just what we needed—no worries or hassles to deal with! We brought our luggage and a carefree mind-set. We made new friends and saw new sights, none of which compared to the beauty and power of the great Niagara Falls.

The waterfall is an unleashed force of power that commands great respect and awe. On the Canadian side, over six hundred thousand gallons of pure aqua-blue, oxygen-rich, white water flow over the ledge of Horseshoe Falls every second. The water falls at thirty-two feet a second, hitting the base of the falls with 2,509 tons of force.[28] The constant roar reveals her force and power. Her beauty is unforgettable, and her power is not to be reckoned with, unless, of course, you want to play with fate!

Our next stop was Amish country, where we visited an authentic working Amish farm. The owners sold hand-stitched quilts, among many other handmade goods. We had visited this town many years prior and had wanted to purchase a quilt, but at that time, we couldn't afford one. Our situation was different now, and I knew the craft of this quilt was something of great value that would be an heirloom to pass down. I also knew that purchasing it would remind me of our trip, and we carefully selected the right one for our cabin.

Bob tried to keep his spirit up, managing fairly well, but was fatigued most of the trip. While riding on the bus, he would sometimes lower his head as if trying to get some relief. We made it through the rest of the week, but he was glad to arrive home.

It was time for round four of chemo, and he was due for lab work to check his liver enzymes. After the labs came back, the oncologist's office called to report that it looked good and to continue his regimen as scheduled.

I had secretly been working on a video of Bob's life that could be used at his funeral service. It profiled his life from infancy through adulthood. I thought, *If you want a great wedding, you have to plan it. And if fate takes the path of death, then I want to have a great funeral for Bob.* I thought it better to spend time planning a funeral that honored his life, and then throw it all away if he did live, than to be caught off guard if he passed away. I wanted to celebrate his life, and the only way to do that was to prepare for it, even through the pain.

I was also working on a scrapbook of his life, and I wrote to our family and friends, asking if they would like to write a note or letter stating something personal about their relationship with Bob. I stated, "If this is too uncomfortable, then write a joke or story you remember him telling or a funny incident you experienced with him." Surprisingly, I received many responses. Some had very personal stories and some were comical, but all were sincere and took you for a walk back in time. I scrapbooked each letter, pulling out details from each story. I couldn't sleep most nights and often stayed up scrapbooking until the early hours of the morning. I tried to stay on a schedule but couldn't, and Bob sometimes slept for days at a time.

After finishing round five of chemo, Bob began to have a slight pressure in his chest where the port was located. I called the doctor and he stated he had no idea what it could be, so we decided to wait to see if it went away. Over the next three weeks, the pressure continued to worsen, and Bob complained again. I called the doctor to let him know the pain had worsened, and he said that he could order a scan, but Bob decided to tough it out a little longer, figuring he would just ask the nurse when he went for his chemo treatment the next week.

When he arrived, the nurse tried to flush his port as usual before injecting the chemo drug. She continued to try for over an hour and finally sought the doctor's advice. The doctor suggested Bob have a scan immediately to see what the problem was. Within a few hours, the results were back, and they showed a blockage in the port line.

The doctor, not wanting Bob to miss his chemo treatment, sent us to the hospital across the street to have a peripherally inserted central catheter (PICC) line put into his upper arm so he could continue receiving chemo without interruption. The PICC line was threaded into a peripheral vein in his upper arm until the catheter tip went into a large vein in his chest near the heart. The inside upper arm is usually the area of choice for a PICC line, which is less invasive than a port.[29] Although the

PICC line carried the risk of susceptibility to infection if used for a long period of time, it enabled a quick resolution to our situation.

Another unfortunate trade-off for having the PICC line was the daily maintenance of flushing out the line with heparin, or saline solution, to prevent clotting. This could be done at home, but the thought of it made me nervous. Before leaving the clinic, the nurse showed me how to clean it, and I realized it was certainly something I could handle, even though I wasn't looking forward to it. After the PICC line was in place, we went back to the doctor's office for Bob's chemo injection. It was a long and exhausting day, and we were ready for it to be over.

Since a port blockage had been found on Bob's scan, and Bob's chest pain was becoming intolerable, we immediately scheduled an appointment with the oncology surgeon who had put the port in. We told him about the ordeal and having the PICC line put in, and he said he would like to see Bob the following morning.

The next morning I knew Bob was in serious trouble; his chest pain was so excruciating that he could hardly get out of bed. I was petrified. I asked if he wanted me to call an ambulance, but he said no. He winced, gritted his teeth, and rolled himself towards the edge of the bed with great difficulty. I worried how I would get him down our long flight of stairs, but we managed by taking one step at a time—I was in front, with him holding on to me all the way down. He made it into the car but winced with every step. In silence, we made the thirty-four-mile drive to the doctor. Bob's body was rigid, and he gritted his teeth in an attempt to deal with the pain.

After the doctor assessed Bob, he suggested that the port be removed immediately, right there in the office. He was still unsure what was causing the complication. Bob was wheeled back to the surgery room. As the doctor prepared to do the procedure, Bob said, "I feel like I'm going to faint."

The doctor said, "Hang on Bob!" as he injected him with a local anesthetic and quickly made an incision in his chest. A stream of blood shot straight up into the air, barely missing the doctor's face, and landed on his lab coat. He instantly jumped back and said, "Whoa!" He removed the catheter, and he could clearly see the blood clot blocking the line. It had been the cause of Bob's severe chest pain. Bob, who was still in great pain, was tremendously relieved to have it out. The doctor finished the procedure, closed the wound, and suggested we schedule another appointment for a new port to be put in the following month.

This was not something we wanted to hear. I questioned why, when Bob had only two more chemo treatments left. The doctor said the PICC line put Bob at a higher risk for infections, and a port would be more advantageous for any future drugs or lab work needed. Even though Bob was dreading it, it was the best thing to do. Bob's journey had its perilous moments, but he was still determined to press on.

While at home recuperating from the ordeal, we heard a knock at the door. Much to our surprise, it was the local family doctor who had originally treated Bob and referred him to our current oncology surgeon. He had moved away but was back in the area and had looked us up. He had heard of Bob's condition and wanted to tell us about a doctor he thought we should see in Gainesville, Georgia, Dr. Ken Dixon. He said, "He is one of the best doctors, an oncology surgeon, and I think he might be able to help you." Bob valued his opinion, so after he left, I immediately called Dr. Dixon's office to schedule an appointment.

The first available appointment was September 22, 2004, and Bob would be nearing completion of his lifetime maximum dosage of Adriamycin and DTIC. We were unsure what would happen when his treatment ended and were anxious to have another option. Proverbs 13:12 says, "Hope deferred makes the heart sick, but when the desire comes, it is a tree of life." And Bob's tree of life had not finished blooming yet!

Bob with new Volkswagen, 2004

Bob and Kim at Niagra Falls, Canada, 2004

Bob and Kim in downtown Savannah, Georgia, 2004

CHAPTER 12

Pressing Towards the Goal

O ver the next several days, while waiting for Dr. Dixon's appointment, Bob mostly slept, and I read books, cooked, gardened, and scrapbooked. Bob's medicines helped alleviate most of his symptoms, but nausea and fatigue were always present. With the exception of our circumstance, living in the cabin was like a permanent vacation. We were so thankful to be able to live there. The view of the Chattahoochee River from every room reminded us that we were surrounded by God's presence. Even if such beauty had not surrounded us, we still would have known God was there. His presence had been undeniable throughout our journey.

The Greek word for *trial* means "to accomplish, to bear, experience, prove, a testing through the idea of piercing." To go through a trial is unwelcome, uncomfortable, challenging, and sometimes unbearable, but a rewarding result can come from it. Christ had to suffer, go through a trial, to give us the result of salvation from the law of sin and death. This was through the Holy Spirit, who also gives us power over our sin and death and gives eternal life. Jesus was tested, He bore and He suffered, He was pierced, and He was proved.

When you go through a trial, you have the opportunity to mature. As James 1:2–5 says, "My brethren, count it all joy when you fall into various trials, knowing that the testing of your faith produces patience. But let patience have its perfect work, that you may be perfect and complete, lacking nothing. If any of you lacks wisdom, let him ask of God, who gives to all liberally and without reproach, and it will be given to him." When you ask, God's wisdom is promised. I asked, "What are my options in this trial? To fall apart, or to stand ready to mature, ready to be used for God's purpose." James 5:11 says, "Indeed we count them blessed who endure. You have heard of the perseverance of Job and seen the end intended by the Lord—that the Lord is very compassionate and merciful."

Isaiah 55:6 reads, "Seek the Lord while He may be found, call upon Him while He is near." Verses 8–9 continue, " 'For My thoughts are not your thoughts, nor are your ways My ways,' says the Lord. 'For as the heavens are higher than the earth, so are My ways higher than your ways, and My thoughts than your thoughts.' " God was mercifully working His plan, and I needed to trust Him.

God's purpose—not my will or experiences—should determine my attitude. God's perspective should determine my point of view, and God's promises should be my motivation. Psalm 62:5–8 says, "My soul, wait silently for God alone, for my expectation is from Him. He only is my rock and my salvation; He is my defense; I shall not be moved. In God is my salvation and my glory; the rock of my strength, and my refuge, is in God. Trust in Him at all times, you people; pour out your heart before Him; God is a refuge for us." When I put expectations on others, I will be disappointed, but when I put my expectations on God, He will never fail me. I must be willing to trust Him.

I had no choice but to go through this challenge. How could I ask God to take this trial away, when I was learning to trust Him, learning to walk by faith, and adding more layers to my spiritual foundation? His Word is truth, and it was in this trial that I could become more Christlike and prove the truthfulness of His Word so that His glory could be revealed.

Hurricane Ivan had hit Pensacola, Florida; and Alabama, and the outskirts of the storm were projected to hit northern Georgia. The unrelenting storm had continued its deadly march across the South, destroying homes, flooding streets, and leaving hundreds of thousands without power. The winds had died down, but we were due to get a lot of rain. As the storm arrived, I began to pace. I wondered how much rain would fall and how high the river would rise. I worried that if Bob were to take a turn for the worse, I would not be able to get him out. How would an ambulance get in the driveway? Mountainous terrain is unforgiving when it comes to rain.

I watched as the river began to rise and its current steadily increased, finally churning the water into a raging torrent. Before the brunt of the storm hit, we packed an overnight bag to prepare for a quick exit if necessary. Some friends, Art and Lou Ann, owned a bed and breakfast on Main Street in downtown Helen and invited us to spend the night until the storm passed. They had befriended us the year before, after purchasing one of our rental cabins, when Bob was first diagnosed. Before the water engulfed our driveway, we took them up on their offer to escape the storm, and we all waited out the storm together. Art naturally exuded a confidence that was rock solid, and his assurance that there was nothing to worry about certainly helped calm my frayed nerves.

The morning after, all was finally calm, and we headed over the bridge to our home. The bridge was still intact, but the streets were littered from the storm's nine inches of rain. We anxiously approached our house and saw our driveway covered with mud, debris, and tree limbs, one that was quite large. Our house was on stilts, and the debris was several feet thick under it. The river had left its mark and without remorse.

Since our driveway was the lowest point in the neighborhood and was at the end of the street, everything flowed downhill towards it. Limbs and sticks had made their way down the grade, slamming against our deck, covering the first three feet of our stairs. The force of the water had even brought an eight-foot tree trunk to rest just short of our deck. The whole area was covered with four inches of wet, slippery red mud, making it even worse. The locals said this was the worst flooding they had seen in forty years.

The AP news said:

> The violent remains of Hurricane Ivan pounded a large swath of the eastern United States on Friday, drenching an area from Georgia to Ohio, washing out dozens of homes, sweeping cars down roadways and trapping more than 100 students at an elementary school. The storm retained its destructive power over land even as its wind speed dropped. Ivan was the deadliest hurricane to hit the United States since Floyd in 1999, but it could have been worse. In all, the hurricane was blamed for 70 deaths in the Caribbean and at least 33 in the United States, 14 of them in Florida.[30]

After seeing the devastation of the area, friends helped to clear a path so we could enter our cabin. A close friend who was also taking care of our lawn maintenance came the next day to clear the remaining logs, debris, and mud. Within days it was back to normal, but Ivan's scars left their mark, physically and in our minds, revealing nature's aggressive power. We had a small storage room on the ground floor, and Ivan's destruction left a muddy watermark approximately two feet high. I recorded it with a permanent black marker, showing the height the water had reached, and wrote, "Hurricane Ivan, 9-04."

It was time for our visit with Dr. Dixon, and we found him to be genuinely professional and sincere. He listened to us, asked some questions, and was graciously honest in making sure we understood our prognosis. His report stated that Bob was doing better than he would have expected and did not look like a man with stage 4 cancer. He commented on his PET scan of eighteen days ago, which showed a "swiss cheese liver." His report further stated:

> Both Mr. and Mrs. Doke attribute a significant amount of his well-being to an herbal medicine I believe called Ambrotose. He has no symptoms of GI bleeding or change in bowel habits, nausea, or vomiting. Some nocturia. On Coumadin 2 mg. a day because of his right port. The left port recently removed and right port now placed yesterday.
>
> I had a lengthy discussion with Mr. and Mrs. Doke today. He is to see me again in two to three weeks. I explained that my attitude toward metastatic malignancies was one that included an aggressive mind-set of local and regional therapies for metastatic cancer to the liver as well as, to some extent, elsewhere. I further explained that clearly he had done better than I would have anticipated had I seen him several

months ago and that I could not tell him what his future course would be.

He responded that he has one further course of Adriamycin left and then has no other immediate options available to him. I would certainly concur. Considerations here would involve resection of this intra-abdominal tumor mass with chemoembolization to the liver. Second would be resection of intra-abdominal mass with installation of hepatic-artery infusion pump. Third would be resection of mass and referral for hepatic total isolation and intraoperative installation of high-dose chemotherapy.

No immediate recommendations made, and I will see him again in two to three weeks. Will talk with his chemo doctor in the meantime.

Ken Dixon, MD

Bob had finished round seven of the chemo and had only one more to go, so we waited for Dr. Dixon's next appointment. During this time, we decided to take a trip and drive up to the northeastern part of the United States. It was early October, the height of fall, and it was a region I had always wanted to explore, especially Vermont and Maine. Bob said, "Let's go!" and insisted he would be just as miserable at home as he would be in a car.

I rejected his suggestion at first, knowing when you don't feel well, you want to be in the comfort of your own home. I wanted desperately to go, even if it was just a driving trip. I was willing if Bob was, but I had to be sure he was up for it, as I was concerned about his stamina. Once again he insisted on the trip, so we loaded up the van and headed out. The thought of experiencing fall up north excited me, even though I knew we couldn't do very much and would be sightseeing from the van.

The first day we made it to West Virginia and stopped at a Hampton Inn. It was one of their star hotels, and they just happened to have a first-class room available because of a cancellation. The hotel offered it to us at the same rate as a regular room, and we didn't think twice about accepting. It had a luxurious king-sized bed—surely a welcome relief for Bob after riding in the car all day. We slept in late, and without an agenda, we continued driving northeastward, enjoying the fall colors along the way.

We stayed on the main highways, sometimes stopping in a quaint town to visit an antique shop or two. The weather was crisp and picture perfect, and the farther north we traveled, the more brilliant the leaves became, as if jumping from a fall-colored palette, contrasting against the bright-blue sky. We passed a small white countryside church, and the fallen leaves formed a vivid carpet of autumn colors that blanketed the lawn. I couldn't resist and pulled over to collect some. We continued through the southern side of Vermont, heading east on Highway 9. My goal was to hit the most southeastern tip of Maine just so I could say I had been there.

After that, I planned our next destination to be Cape Cod in Massachusetts. While on the Cape, I drove out to Hyannis Port late that afternoon. The weather was clear, the ocean deep blue, and the Cape's white homes stood out in vivid contrast. I couldn't stop admiring the architecture, driving through neighborhoods and taking in every detail, along with the ocean views whenever they became visible. Being a native Floridian, I pondered, *God is so detailed! Every region is so uniquely diverse— the weather, the foliage, the ocean, the architecture. New England has its own unique identity, and I love it!*

It was late afternoon. I knew the sun would soon be setting, so we decided to head inland. Before leaving, we stopped at a neighborhood common area to stretch. A local fellow was passing by, and I asked if he knew where the Kennedy compound was. He pointed to the area but explained it was not visible anymore. So we savored the fresh salt air and view of the deep-blue sea once more before heading westward and stopping for the night.

Our next destination was upstate New York. We had visited New York City in the eighties, but I had always heard upstate New York was very different. With no route in mind, we continued on, and by sheer happenstance, we drove through the vicinity of West Point Military Academy. The countryside was so picturesque! I wanted to capture the panoramic view that my eyes were taking in, but I knew a picture wouldn't do it justice. I so desperately wanted to stop and tour the academy, but thought, *It's okay. Perhaps I can return someday.*

Pennsylvania Dutch country and Gettysburg National Military Park were next on our trip. We went to the Gettysburg Visitor Center and discovered that a licensed guide was available for hire, so we spent the day getting a private history lesson right in our car.

The Battle of Gettysburg was a turning point in the Civil War, the Union victory in the summer of 1863 that ended General Robert E. Lee's second and most ambitious invasion of the North. Often referred to as the "High Water Mark of the Rebellion," it was the war's bloodiest battle, with fifty-one thousand casualties. The Union's Army of the Potomac, long the nemesis of Lee's forces in Virginia, met the Confederate invasion at the town of Gettysburg, under the command of Major General George Gordon Meade. The Northerners fought with a desperation not often seen before at other battlefields. Despite initial Confederate success, the battle turned against Lee on July 3, 1863, and with few options remaining to him, the general ordered his army back to Virginia. The Union victory at the Battle of Gettysburg resulted not only in Lee's retreat to Virginia, but in an end to the hopes of the

Confederacy for independence. It also provided President Abraham Lincoln with the setting for his most famous speech, the Gettysburg Address.[31]

After Pennsylvania, we returned home. In all, we traveled over 2,300 miles in nine days! Bob was glad to have seen that part of the country, but he was also glad to return home.

It was time to start round eight of chemo, the last and final round. Bob was due for a CT scan to determine if there had been any progress. The tests revealed that the chemo had not worked, and the inferior vena cava, the large vein that drains directly into the heart after gathering incoming blood from the body, was thinning. Adriamycin was noted to be toxic to the heart and to accumulate in your system, thus the prescription of eight rounds being the lifetime dose.

Just after finishing, Bob suffered pain in the upper right quadrant of his chest that radiated into his right shoulder. Dr. Dixon suggested it was a liver infarction. If so, the liver tissue had died, causing hemorrhage and an accumulation of blood in the area. He said, "If you have any extreme pain, you need to go directly to the emergency room"; and in a monotone voice, he followed up with, "Bob, you could die from this." He was gently preparing us, and I appreciated his truthful words.

Bob was already taking oxycodone for pain management, so having to deal with more pain was not welcome. The doctor also instructed him to stop taking Coumadin, a blood thinner. Fearful thoughts raced through our minds: *This really could be the end.*

With all the odds against Bob, every day was a gift, and we constantly lived with that in the forefront of our minds. We also had peace if it was the end. The Lord promised He would be with us always, even through the valley of the shadow of death. God did not say He would be with us through death, because He conquered death. Death is a transition only—from one plane to

140

another. When we die, our bodies go back to the earth, but as Christians, our spirits shift from earth to heaven. Thankfully, Bob's pain did not worsen, thus avoiding a trip to the emergency room.

Meanwhile, Dr. Dixon consulted with a radiology-department chief on what course of action to take next. This doctor felt that Bob should have chemoembolization of the liver first, a process where radioactive beads would be injected into his circulatory system to deliver targeted radiation to the tumor in his liver. After this procedure, his stomach mass would be resected. Dr. Dixon agreed; however, he had concerns that the resection might make Bob's cancer grow faster. We scheduled an initial consultation for the chemoembolization and planned to discuss the resection with Dr. Dixon at a later date.

Before we knew whether Bob was a candidate for chemoembolization, he needed an arteriogram. An arteriogram is a diagnostic test that involves viewing the arteries and/or attached organs by injecting a contrast medium, or dye, into the artery and taking an X-ray.[32] The aim of the arteriogram was to see if the dye flowed into the liver and not into the lungs. Only a small percentage was allowed to flow into the lungs, and anything over that amount was not acceptable and would rule out the possibility of having the procedure done. Bob's results came back with only 4 percent shunting to the lungs, so he could have the procedure. It was scheduled to take place three weeks later.

While home recuperating from the arteriogram, Bob began to have pain in his foot. It continued over the next few days and became acute, so I called his doctor. He suggested it could be a blood clot from the arteriogram procedure and recommended going to the nearest emergency room. So we did.

While in a room separated by curtains, I could hear a young girl next to us crying while on the phone. She was pleading not to be put into another foster home. A technician came in to take Bob to get an X-ray, and I wondered what might become of her, hoping she would still be there when we returned.

To my surprise she was, but now a nurse was trying to console her. The girl explained that she didn't want to go to another foster home, especially in Cleveland. The nurse tried to convince her everything would be okay, but it was to no avail. The phone rang, and I could hear the girl saying, "Please don't make me go. The kids are mean there; they'll make fun of me. I'll just run away!"

I understood her fear and frustration at being unable to control her situation, but I knew there was hope. Bob and I had felt that way so many times throughout our medical journey. I wanted to open the curtain and talk to her, but I knew the timing was not right. I began to pray and asked the Lord to make a way for me to speak with her.

Bob's doctor came in with a diagnosis of "pain in limb," and wrote a prescription for six hundred milligrams of Motrin and discharged us. We were so thankful it wasn't a blood clot!

As we left, passing the girl's curtain, I urgently prayed, *God make a way for me to get to that girl—make a way!* Just as we walked past, I looked back, believing God would make a way. At that moment, the girl peered out from her cubicle. I immediately turned and ran to her. I grabbed her hands and emphatically said, "I was next door to you and heard every word you said." I was literally shaking inside, and my voice was filled with a power that could come only from the Holy Spirit. I asked, "What is your name?"

She said, "Paitra," and big tears began to flow down her cheeks. She hugged me tightly and didn't want to let go.

I hugged her with all my might while speaking in her ear: "God loves you so much! And He cares about your every need." Then I asked if she had a Bible, and she said yes. I told her to read Psalm 139 to see just how special she was to God. He knew her before she was even born, and He knew who she was going to become. I said, "It doesn't matter what anyone thinks of you—only what God thinks of you—and please do not run away. You don't need any more trouble than you already have."

She looked at me intently, taking it all in, her eyes still filled with tears. I encouraged her to be obedient to those who were over her, as long as they were not hurting her, and that God would honor her if she did. Before I departed, we hugged once again.

As I walked down the hall, God prompted me to turn around and give her a bookmark of scriptures I had been working on for myself. I found a seat for Bob, promising to return quickly, and ran back to her. This time I didn't wait for her to open the curtain; with boldness I opened it, and much to my surprise, she had a Bible open and was searching for Psalm 139. My heart leaped for joy!

I helped her find the psalm and then shared Bob's diagnosis and our trial. This time tears were in my eyes as I told her how he was dying of cancer. Despite our earthly struggles, God had been our help and comfort; He had given us strength and peace to get through. Then I wrote my name and phone number on a piece of paper and told her to call me if she got into a situation where she was afraid or needed help. I knew I needed to get back to Bob, so we hugged and I left. What transpired that night confirmed that God was using our situation. What could have been an unfortunate event turned out to be an opportunity to minister and testify to His unconditional love.

The radioactive beads used in Bob's chemoembolization were called SIR-Spheres. They are tiny polymer (plastic) beads (about one-third the diameter of a strand of hair) that are combined with Y90 (yttrium-90), a radioisotope that emits pure beta radiation. This isotope is attached to microscopic spheres that deliver the radiotherapy to the tumor. Yttrium-90 has a half-life of about sixty-four hours, which means that every sixty-four hours the level of radiation falls by one-half until it is effectively gone after two weeks.

When discussing the specifics of the procedure, the doctor said, "Mr. Doke, make sure you show up!"

We looked at him with a puzzled look and said, "Of course, why would we not?"

Smiling, he continued, "We have to express ship these beads overnight from Australia, and you need to be here the morning they arrive." Then he said, "And they cost $20,000!"

We replied, "In that case, we'll get a hotel room in the area to make sure we are here."

He continued, "This will be an outpatient procedure done under local sedation in the radiology department. A small incision will be made in your groin, and a flexible catheter will be positioned into the liver under X-ray guidance to allow for infusion of the beads into your liver tumor. The procedure should last about one hour, and you should be discharged within twenty-four hours."

A nuclear-medicine scan was to be done before the spheres were administered to assure that the catheter was correctly positioned and that the tumor was properly targeted. During the procedure, an interventional radiologist would selectively catheterize the arteries feeding the tumor and monitor the catheter during administration of the dose.

The precautions after the procedure were extensive. For the first week after treatment, you could not travel on public transportation, sit next to a fellow passenger for more than two hours, sleep in the same bed with another person, have close contact with children or pregnant women, and could have close contact with other adults for only a few minutes at a time. For prolonged periods of interaction, individuals were advised to stay more than six feet away for the first three days.

Liver tumors are hypervascular and derive most of their blood supply from the hepatic artery, while healthy liver tissue is fed predominantly by the portal vein. After the SIR-Spheres are injected into the hepatic artery supplying blood to the tumor, the beads become lodged in the tumor and destroy the cancer cells by delivering beta radiation for approximately two weeks. SIR-Spheres are considered a regional treatment, as the radiation is directed to the liver and does not affect the other organs in the body as conventional radiation does. The dose of radiation in conjunction with its proximity to the tumor destroys the tumor and preserves the healthy liver tissue. SIR-Spheres are generally not regarded as a cure but have been shown to shrink the tumor more than chemotherapy alone.[33]

It was a month before Christmas and time for the chemoembolization. After having the preprocedure to verify that Bob was a candidate, we knew what to expect because the procedure would be similar. We arrived two hours early for his 10:30 a.m. appointment, as requested. After waiting four hours, a technician finally came for Bob at 12:15 p.m.

Three hours passed; I was still sitting in the waiting room and had not been given an update on Bob or the procedure. I asked the receptionist if she could tell me what Bob's status was, and she told me I could go into the IV room to see him. I walked in, thinking the procedure was finished, but soon realized it had not even started.

When I saw Bob lying there with the IV still in his arm, waiting for the procedure, I was beside myself! He looked so weary. Even on a good day, Bob was fragile, and in preparation for the procedure, he had not eaten since midnight the night before. I knew how hungry and weak he must be. We weren't given any explanation for the delay, and I felt we deserved some answers. Soon after, around four o'clock, they came to take him for the procedure, and I went back to the waiting room. I couldn't believe that a patient would have to wait an entire day for what was supposed to be an hour-long procedure, let alone a patient who was already medically challenged.

Five o'clock approached, and I was the only one left in the waiting room, worried and pacing. At 5:45 p.m. the doctor finally came out and said, "He's out, but we had a little problem. The radioactive beads were put into saline solution instead of sterile water, but I immediately switched them to sterile water and injected them very fast to get them all in." He also called the medical director for Sirtex for additional advice, and they said to monitor Bob's blood, renal function, and urine for radioactivity.

There was no doubt now that we would be staying the night. Already upset, I felt my heart sink, and I wondered, *What does this really mean? Has the radioactivity on the beads been compromised? How will this affect Bob's condition? Could it cause more harm than expected? How could this mishap happen?* I went in to see him after the procedure, and he lay there awake and looking totally helpless. He was relying on the doctors and didn't have any control over their actions. I was afraid, angry, and confused. Bob was docile, dependent, and hungry. All he wanted to know was when he could have a meal.

We were assigned a room that had a portable bed for me to sleep on. Our postop instructions were to stay six feet away from each other, and I wondered if my cot was too close to Bob's bed. When I asked about this, the doctor smiled and said, "No, it's just babies that need to be kept that far away."

All throughout the night, the nurse came in for urine and blood samples. The radiation measurements in his urine were 60 percent when first collected but diminished to 10 percent by morning. The following morning a test was performed to assess his renal function. We were told the test results were acceptable enough for Bob to be discharged. After lunch we were finally released and were more than eager to get home.

It was recommended that Bob have ongoing analysis of his platelet and white-blood-cell (WBC) counts over the next few weeks to detect any changes in bone marrow. Proverbs 18:14 says, "The spirit of a man can endure his sickness, but a broken spirit who can bear?" (NASB). My spirit was breaking, and I knew Bob's was too. Our experience with this procedure had not been positive. The lack of professionalism before and during the procedure, along with having the responsibility of being Bob's sole caregiver, had left my frustration at an all-time high.

Not long after becoming Bob's caregiver, I realized that the health-care system was changing. No longer could you feel secure and put your faith and total trust in your doctor, nurse, or technician. I learned to have my guard up. The burden of knowing best practices and quality care had shifted from the professionals to the patients and their caregivers. It was imperative that I learn to be proactive in Bob's health care, to learn about his disease, procedures, and medicines. Results are obviously the goal of medical treatment, but I learned that patient sensitivity, professionalism, and cleanliness were sometimes compromised to get them.

Christmas was just a few weeks away, and family and friends were making plans to spend it with us. I ached for Bob, who was lethargic and not eating much after that last medical episode. If he showed the slightest bit of interest in a food, I would run to the local market in Helen and purchase it. It delighted me to make something I thought he would eat, but after two bites, he would put it down. I longed for him to eat, to get some nourishment, but there was nothing I could do other than to pray.

I prayed for God to hold on to him, to wrap His loving arms around him, to be with him as he walked through this valley, and to lift his spirit even though his body was wasting away. I prayed for God to let him soar as high as the eagle, to feel no pain, to have His peace, and to experience the joy that comes from knowing the Lord. The Lord heard my prayer and answered it. Psalm 139:4 declares, "Even before there is a word on my tongue, behold, O Lord, You know it all" (NASB). Bob clearly displayed God's peace, and it was evident to all who were around him that Christmas.

I was doing a Bible study via e-mail with several ladies, some local and some in other states. The Bible study was by Elizabeth George, and it was called "A Woman's Walk with God—Growing in the Fruit of the Spirit." I didn't realize it until later, but that study was my support group. As each of us wrote our responses to the Bible-study questions, we were not only learning God's Word, but we were encouraging each other as well. We were also developing our characters to become more Christlike. As Galatians 5:22–25 says, "But the fruit of the Spirit is love, joy, peace, longsuffering, kindness, goodness, faithfulness, gentleness, self-control. Against such there is no law. And those who are Christ's have crucified the flesh with its passions and desires. If we live in the Spirit, let us also walk in the Spirit."

The Greek translation for *living* in the Spirit is "point of time, moment, to prick, to mark (incise or punch) for recognition of ownership, i.e., scar of service." I thought of each of these meanings and the fruit of my life. Perhaps the fruit of our lives (our behavior, what we have done) is a mark, or prick, in time and space, a mark incised on others' lives. Some of us make a mark (leave memories) in just one heart, some in many hearts, and some are so well remembered that others erect memorials such as streets, buildings, bridges, or statues named in their honor. Life is full of pain, wounds, and trials that leave emotional and physical scars. A scar is the memorial. It's history—it happened!

You enter into time and space simply by being born; that is your very first mark. Then, throughout your life, you and those around you acquire new marks with every deed. Your marks are incised on people's hearts and recorded for recognition by God, to be used for His glory or for His judgment. As Ecclesiastes 12:14 says, "For God will bring every act to judgment, everything which is hidden, whether it is good or evil" (NASB); and 2 Timothy 4:1 adds, "I charge you therefore before God and the Lord Jesus Christ, who will judge the living and the dead at His appearing and His kingdom."

What matters most in life is what you have done for the Lord. If you are pleasing Him, then you automatically please mankind. Have you loved enough, being His hands and feet to a lost and dying world? Have you evangelized enough, telling His gospel message of life, death, resurrection, and hope? Have you crucified your flesh (your will) enough, putting your sinful desires to death, so His Holy Spirit can live through you? Have you accepted His grace enough, so you can experience abundant life in your soul? Have you been bold enough to be able to tell others the truth, even in the face of rejection, that they are going down a wrong road or that they are nothing without Him, and that they need a Savior?

The fact that He is the only God who came down to earth, fully man and yet fully God, and died on a cross with over five hundred witnesses gives Him the right to say, "I am the only way!" John 14:6 declares, "I am the way, the truth, and the life. No man comes to the Father except through Me."

Just as we are all born, we all must face death. The Bible tells us we are like the flower that fades. Our life is like a breath—here one minute, gone the next. Isaiah 40:6–7 says, "All flesh is grass, and all its loveliness is like the flower of the field. The grass withers, the flower fades." James 4:14–15 says, "Whereas you do not know what will happen tomorrow. For what is your life? It is even a vapor that appears for a little time and then vanishes away. Instead you ought to say, 'If the Lord wills, we shall live and do this or that.'" It is evident that the next day, or even the next breath, is not promised, so why would you not want to make the most of every day?

Bob was thankful for every minute, and the mark he incised will not be forgotten in his generation or the one that follows, as he lives on through the stories told of the love, joy, and wisdom he imparted. Bob knew the mark he was imprinting onto other's hearts would eventually fade as generations passed. He also knew that what we do for God's glory never fades!

Tree trunk that landed under the house—Hurricane Ivan, 2004

**Chattahoochee River flooding, leaving debris and mud
—Hurricane Ivan, 2004**

Chattahoochee River's destruction—Hurricane Ivan, 2004

Bob with brother Glenn and sister Cindy, Christmas, 2004

CHAPTER 13

The Tumor Is Winning!

B ob's energy level was declining, and his doctor put him on Ritalin. Ritalin is used in children for attention deficit hyperactivity disorder (ADHD), but in adults it increases mental alertness. It helped for about a month, but as the cancer spread, the effectiveness of the Ritalin decreased. The stomach tumor was so large it caused Bob to look eight months pregnant, and it literally took all of his nourishment as it grew, leaving his body malnourished. The tumor even had its own blood supply. Bob continued to lose weight, but he was managing to hold on.

January arrived and with it our follow-up PET scan and subsequent office visit. Upon arrival, instead of us waiting like usual, the nurse took us back to the doctor's private office. Upon entering, the doctor exuberantly stood up and smiled, beaming from ear to ear. We quickly exchanged greetings, and then he blurted out, "It worked! The scans revealed the results we had hoped for." He explained that the liver showed 95 percent cell death.

Previously he had suggested that there might be an option for Bob to have one more liver chemoembolization, assuring death of the cancerous liver cells, but after seeing the results, he didn't think it would be necessary. Bob's whole countenance changed! We joked and laughed and then discussed shifting Bob's care to Dr. Dixon.

After we left, Bob's emotions welled up. When we got into the breezeway, he grinned, and with tear-filled eyes, he kicked up his heels with all the energy he could muster and said, "It worked, it worked!" Then he phoned family and friends to tell them the great news.

I knew that having 95 percent cell death meant he was living on only 5 percent of his liver. I wondered, *How long can you live on five percent?* but I dared not say anything and deflate his excitement. He was rejoicing, and I rejoiced with him, even though I knew this was not a permanent solution. Behind my smile, my heart was breaking.

Next we saw Dr. Dixon to discuss the possible resection of the stomach mass. Having such positive results from the radioactive SIR-Spheres beads gave Bob the hope he needed to get through the upcoming surgery. He was ready! He knew his options were ending, and he knew that if he were to die in surgery, he would welcome it because it would be a painless way to go. Dr. Dixon was not hasty to schedule surgery and ordered several tests to determine Bob's odds. He proceeded cautiously and wrote, "I think Bob has a good one-in-three chance that he could either die in the postoperative period or be worsened by the surgery." Bob knew this aggressive procedure was his last chance at trying to cheat death a little longer, and Dr. Dixon knew it was necessary to get Bob some relief.

The size of Bob's stomach tumor had begun affecting his breathing. His feet were swelling, and he looked ten months pregnant. The MRI measured the tumor at 17 by 23 centimeters (6.7 inches by 9 inches). One Sunday, while sitting in his chair, he told my mom before she left for church, "Don't forget to pray!" She responded, "Bob, the church has never stopped." Family and friends had been relentlessly praying, not just in Georgia, but in other states as well.

One of the doctor's reports read, "He is still vigorous, but clearly tumor is progressing." Dr. Dixon knew we had a small window of opportunity and noted that Bob was going downhill. His report stated:

> His CT originally to me did not look as bad as described on the radiology report, but on further review and reflection, there is a large amount of tumor in the liver. Some of it has clearly been affected by the SIRS therapy, but there is a large amount of active tumor in a bilobar multinodular fashion. Perhaps he would be benefited by debulking of his abdominal tumor, but this would be 50-50 about whether it would make him better or not in my view.

After noting in his report how Bob's labs had showed a decline in health, he stated:

> The portal vein, although compressed by this tumor, does go in a hepatopetal fashion, though I do not think his deteriorating liver function is due to portal venous thrombosis. Perhaps there is increasing tumor that we are misreading, but I am hopeful that debulking the abdominal tumor will result in some reversal of this course. This is a patient who has his terminal ileum and right and transverse colon involved by tumor, but also for surgery to consist of removal of intra-abdominal tumor mass, and probable resection of the colon with ileo-descending colostomy.

Risks and indications have been discussed with the patient and his wife on multiple occasions. After a lengthy discussion, the patient and his wife have understood the attempt of this operation to diminish symptoms and extend life with no possibility of cure. They do understand that there is a real risk of him dying in the postoperative period and that the surgery, instead of helping, may hurt. However, he is understanding of these issues and strongly desires to proceed.

It was time for surgery, and Bob was admitted a day early, February 10, 2005, to have two units of fresh plasma injected to correct his abnormal clotting and to have a bowel prep. It was the most anxious day of our lives. Bob's sister, Cindy, had flown in from Fort Lauderdale the day before. Since we lived forty-five minutes from Gainesville, where the operation was being performed, she checked into a nearby hotel, and I stayed with her so we could be close to the hospital.

My pastor, church staff, immediate family, and dear friends came to the hospital early the next morning in time to pray with Bob before surgery. It was a special moment as we all gathered around him, held hands, and prayed. You could feel the seriousness of the moment, but you could also feel God's presence, power, and Spirit. No matter what the odds were, we knew it would be all right; it was all in God's hands, and He knew best.

We all stood in the hallway as Bob's gurney disappeared down the hall. Then we made our way to the hospital's main-lobby waiting area. Our children's pastor brought a wicker cloth-lined laundry basket filled with bottled water, soft drinks, crackers, gum, and all sorts of candy. It was a welcome surprise and a delight to see.

It was 9:15 a.m., and I was told Bob's surgery was estimated to be about five hours long. The possible outcomes of surgery were that he would most likely be on life support, have a feeding tube and/or a colostomy bag, that the tumor could be attached to other organs, that one-half of Bob's stomach would be removed, that his stamina would run out, that his heart could stop. As we waited, we engaged in multiple lighthearted conversations. It was as though we were all lifted up by the Holy Spirit, anxious, but fully trusting God and feeling His peace in the midst of it.

Periodically the doctor notified me via phone that they were still operating and all was going well. Four hours into the operation, I was surprised to be summoned to the surgery area. I hurriedly followed the directions to get there, with family following behind. Dr. Dixon entered the room with a split-second smile that quickly turned serious. He said, "Bob made it!"

He drained six liters of ascites (fluid); removed a nodule in the pelvic area; resected the tumor mass, part of the liver, the right and transverse colon with ileocolostomy, and half the stomach (a full-thickness gastrectomy); repaired his umbilical hernia; and his bowels were replaced with care to ensure there was no kinking. He lost about two liters of blood. The good news was there was no need to resuscitate, no life support, no colostomy bag, no feeding tube, the tumor was not attached to other organs as supposed, and the surgery took only four hours instead of five.

After pausing, and with a stoic look, Dr. Dixon said, "But Bob's not out of the woods yet—his tank is out of gas." I knew he could still die, but I knew God wasn't finished with this trial yet. He wouldn't have allowed the surgery to go so well just to end it all.

Bob was taken to ICU, and we were told he could be there for up to two weeks. The doctor stated Bob's surgery would be treated like someone who had gastric bypass surgery: his meals would need to be small. The focus was to get Bob's strength up. As a result of the extensive surgery, his internal fluid levels were unbalanced, and he had anemia. He was given two more units of blood.

The next several days were a struggle as Bob fought edema in the lower extremities and ascites, an abnormal accumulation of fluid in the spaces between tissue and organs in the abdominal cavity. He beat the odds again. Just two days after surgery, he was moved to a regular room. A student nurse came to visit and shared that she had observed Bob's surgery. She surprisingly explained, "In nursing school, I was taught that tumors are a grayish color, but Bob's had colors like a rainbow." I thought how God's beauty could be revealed even in something so ugly. Just like He did with the rainbow that appeared before our car, He was confirming, "I'm still here!"

The area around Bob's catheter started to swell, and after a few hours, his arm was twice its size. The swelling started to move into his whole body. He had been on Lasix and Aldactone to prevent swelling, but something had changed, and they didn't seem to be working. The doctor was very concerned and increased his dose. They continued to monitor him frequently. His compromised body was battling the effects of surgery as well as it could. So much was out of his control.

I put a sign on Bob's door that said "No Visitors" to allow him to rest, and I occasionally stepped outside to talk with family, friends, or the sympathetic nurses. The nurses understood how fragile and precious each moment with Bob was as they ticked by, and they witnessed and marveled at God's power in our lives. I sometimes exposed my broken heart to them, often tearing up. I also shared with them how the Lord had been with us throughout our whole trial, how He was holding us up, and no matter what happened, we were blessed to know our loving Father, Jehovah God, and to be able to spend our lives together for the years we had been given. The nurses were superb, emotionally supportive, and became our best friends.

Ten days after surgery, Bob was finally able to have a liquid diet. His body was still swelling from ascites, and his stomach had started to distend. After running a test, it was discovered he had a kink in his bowel. The doctor said, "It could work itself out." It wasn't an option to have another surgery, so we prayed, waited, and two days later it went back into position. Praise the Lord!

It had been a tiresome week, and I decided to go home to exchange some clothes and check on things. A thunderstorm had just come through Helen, and the electricity was off. It was late afternoon, so I quickly grabbed what I needed and left. I hated leaving Bob, even though it was just for a little while. It began to flash lightning again, so I darted to my parents' house about eight miles away to take shelter until the storm passed. Previous storms had taken a toll on me, and I found they were making me extremely anxious. This storm was not subsiding, and it was nearing nine o'clock. Bob called to tell me to stay put until the storm passed; then his voice cracked. Fear entered us both as we considered that he could die before I returned.

While I was still on the phone debating with Bob if I should drive through the storm, an old friend, Dennis, peered into his room. Bob's response conveyed instant security. God was providing again! It helped calm my nerves because I knew Bob was comforted. We both agreed that I would wait for the storm to pass. It continued late into the night, and I drifted to sleep, getting up at 4 a.m. to return to the hospital. Bob was a welcome sight when I entered his room.

Things were looking up. A few days later, Bob was able to get up, take a shower, and even walk a bit. Three days after that, he was discharged. It had been a fifteen-day ordeal, and his body was still swollen. Just as he had gotten used to living with a tumor, he would now have to adjust to this new postsurgery level of existence. It would be difficult, but we were going home!

CHAPTER 14

God's Call to Minister

W e had been home about two weeks and were busy trying to balance all of Bob's medicines and the swelling. He was stable, but we knew his health could take a turn at any moment. My friend Gloria had recently put her mom in a nursing home in Port Richey, Florida, and called to tell me she had received news that her mom was in serious condition. Gloria was upset because she had no one to drive with her. It was more than an eight-hour-long trip, and she didn't want to go alone. For me to go was not even considered, so I consoled her the best I could and said good-bye.

While watching television, Bob asked, "What did Gloria want?" I explained, and after a moment of silence, he looked at me and said, "You need to go."

I looked at him like he was crazy and said, "Oh no! I'm not leaving you. It would tear me up if something happened and I was not here with you." I knew if I went, fear and doubt would set in when I crossed the state line, and I could not handle that. I knew the enemy would put thoughts in my head: *You shouldn't have left. What if he dies?*

But Bob said it again, "You need to take your friend to see her mom."

I hesitated, but deep down I knew the Lord was speaking through him. I firmly replied, "Okay, I will go only because I have no doubt that this is from the Lord. I'll call our parents to see if they can take care of you, and if they can, I will go."

I called Gloria back to tell her the good news, and she almost didn't believe me. She was overjoyed! She too knew it had to be the Lord speaking through Bob and assured me that if we got to Florida and Bob needed me, she would drive us back. We were filled with the peace of God that surpasses all of man's natural understanding. My decision required total trust and was not easy to do. But I knew God, and He would reward our faithfulness. God knew I was honoring Him through the fact that I was honoring my husband to go.

Philippians 1:6 says, "Being confident of this very thing, that He who has begun a good work in you will complete it until the day of Jesus Christ." Gloria knew her mom was a Christian, and if she needed to leave her to bring me back, it would be okay. She knew where her mom was going to spend eternity; her spirit was secure.

We left the next afternoon and arrived at her brother's house around 11 p.m. without incident. Even though it was late, we picked him up and went to the hospital to see their mother. Gloria had taken care of her mom for the past three and a half years because she had Alzheimer's. Recently her mother had been moved to a nursing home near Gloria's brother and sister in Florida. When we arrived, her mother was barely coherent, and we gathered around her bed to console her.

Before Gloria's mother moved to Florida, her abilities had deteriorated to the point of barely being able to sing "Jesus Loves Me." It was her mother's favorite song, and Gloria had continued singing and mouthing the words, filling in the blanks when her mother forgot. That night around her bed, we sang "Jesus Loves Me," and her mother mouthed some of the words, even though no voice was heard. It was a very special moment. We held her hand a while longer, kissed her forehead, and left.

The next morning I called to check on Bob, and he sounded good. I think he was actually enjoying some time alone. Between family and friends, he was well taken care of. Gloria had gone outside and realized her tire was flat, so her nephew changed it and we left for the hospital.

It was a long day, and I decided to find a gift for Gloria's mother while the doctor discussed her prognosis with the family. Searching in the hospital gift shop, unsure of what to purchase because of her critical condition, I came across a little white stuffed lamb. Gloria and I had started collecting stuffed lambs to use for teaching Sunday school. This one just happened to play "Jesus Loves Me." I was astonished when I turned the key and heard that song but knew once again the Lord had provided. Even in her mother's state, when I put that lamb by her ear, she would mouth the words.

Surgery was not an option for Gloria's mother because her colon had gangrene, so the doctor said hospice would be best. He said he would try to find a hospice room in the area, but he was not optimistic. After a few minutes, he returned with a smile. "We've got a room nearby," he said, and it was a nice one. After taking a break to eat, we returned to the hospital and visited for a while longer, discussing final arrangements. The ambulance arrived, and we followed it to her mother's new room and helped her settle in before leaving for the night.

The next morning I made one of my many calls to Bob, and this time I was met with a fearful voice on the other end. Even though he tried to assure me he was okay, I could tell he was trying to mask his true feelings. I handed the phone to Gloria so she could say hello and hear it too. She said, "Kim, it's time. Let me go say bye to my mom, and then I'll take you home." She was being true to her word and would follow through with her promise no matter what.

She told her brother about our plans to leave that afternoon, and we all decided to meet in the hospice waiting area before going in to see her mom. Gloria and her siblings prepared themselves to say good-bye, and they each took turns going into her room. After they finished, Gloria asked if I wanted to see her too. I did. The nurse had started giving her mother morphine under her tongue, so she was incoherent. Nevertheless, it was a sweet and teary day, and Gloria readied herself to leave. It was getting late, and I was growing very anxious. I knew if we left now we would arrive home close to midnight, but the circumstances warranted it.

The journey home was long. Halfway home, our engine started acting up, and we could go only about forty miles an hour on the interstate. The car would intermittently speed up and then fall back again. We were petrified! I began to pray and encouraged Gloria to pray as well. God had not failed us and had worked throughout the whole weekend: our tire didn't blow until getting to her brother's, I found that lamb, God opened the door for her mother's nearby hospice room, and Gloria's brother and sister had reunited after several years of estrangement. We had too much proof to distrust God now.

The car continued to act up, but we made it home. Even though it was well after midnight, Bob came down the stairs to greet us, and it was a welcome sight for us both. The next morning Gloria called to say she had another flat tire. We couldn't believe it, and we praised and thanked the Lord as we marveled at His providence once again.

CHAPTER 15

Uncharted Days

‿✑

"**B**eloved, do not think it strange concerning the fiery trial which is to try you, as though some strange thing happened to you; but rejoice to the extent that you partake of Christ's sufferings, that when His glory is revealed, you may also be glad with exceeding joy" (1 Peter 4:12–13).

After the surgery, Bob was having significant pain below his rib cage, and the swelling continued. The pain was due to bleeding in his liver, and the swelling was from fluid buildup (ascites). After Bob's doctor conferred with two other doctors, it was concluded that Bob had portal hypertension and needed a TIPS (transjugular intrahepatic portosystemic shunt) procedure. TIPS is a radiological procedure in which a stent (a tubular device) is placed in the middle of the liver to reroute the blood flow.[34]

Knowing that Bob would need to stay in ICU after the procedure, we stayed in the area at a Hampton Inn. My mother also came to keep me company and provide support. We checked in at 7:30 a.m. for the procedure, and Bob was given presurgery plasma. The procedure was finished by 3:35 p.m. The doctor came out to say it had gone well, but that Bob would need to stay in ICU a few days to ensure no fluid went to his brain or lungs.

The next morning we arrived to find Bob sitting up and alert. The nurse said he was being released. I thought, *Released to a regular room?* But I was wrong—he was going home! We left late that afternoon and stayed at the hotel one more night to be nearby just in case there were any complications. I couldn't believe it; we had beat the odds again!

Bob's diagnosis of portal hypertension was especially concerning because encephalopathy can occur. This is where blood flow is diverted away from the liver, causing confusion and forgetfulness. I pondered what might come next. Thankfully, Bob never had these symptoms and remained alert most of the time, even when taking his pain medications.

We continued Bob's care, having ultrasounds, labs, his port flushed, and doctors' appointments to the oncologist and Dr. Dixon to monitor his meds and progress. After the TIPS procedure, the ascites did improve, and Bob continued taking spironolactone and Lasix to keep it under control. His lab report came back with fair results, considering his condition. A one-month follow-up PET scan was due after the TIPS procedure. After that was a ten-week follow-up ultrasound. Even though Bob was doing relatively well, he had little energy. His weight was down to 170 pounds, but that consisted also of fluid within his abdomen. His waist measured thirty-nine inches.

We went to Tallahassee to spend a few days with family, but Bob stayed in bed the whole time, so we returned home. Bob's doctors considered opening his shunt further to allow more protein to come through. This would be very dangerous, since it could cause fluid to go to the brain and cause disorientation, so they ruled it out. To us these were scary and uncharted days, but not to God. As Psalm 139:1–4 so eloquently says, "O

Lord, You have searched me and known me. You know when I sit down and when I rise up; You understand my thought from afar. You scrutinize my path and my lying down, and are intimately acquainted with all my ways. Even before there is a word on my tongue, behold, O Lord, You know it all" (NASB). And Psalm 31:3 further says, "For You are my rock and my fortress; therefore, for Your name's sake, lead me and guide me."

CHAPTER 16

Forever My Hero

It was time for the annual Relay for Life in Cleveland, and Bob wanted to go. We had previously attended the survivors' dinner, and he had really enjoyed it. He was also proud that he was beating the odds by being alive. He wanted to go to Relay for Life to make that first victory lap and prove it.

The opening lap was for all the cancer survivors, and Bob beamed from ear to ear as he made his way to join the others. After beginning the first lap, he realized he was too weak to finish. He pushed himself to round the bend and a golf-cart driver quickly came to his aid. He gladly climbed on board, allowing him to finish the lap. Bob flashed his beaming smile while waving to those applauding on the sidelines. It was a heart-wrenching moment with many tear-filled eyes.

The caregivers were honored with an etched Christmas ornament, a keepsake to remember the memorable event. Every Christmas, as I hang it on my tree, I am reminded of Bob's bravery and perseverance.

It was still cool out, so we decided to take a day trip to Rock City in Tennessee. Bob's mom had always wanted to go, especially since she had a "See Rock City" bird-house, so we invited her to come along. Since we lived in the mountains, there wasn't a direct route, so we opted for the most scenic route, US Route 64. This route was where the Olympic white-water competition was held in 1996. Along this route, you see spectacular views of mountains, streams, rivers, lakes, and occasionally you may even catch some white-water rafters, tubers, or kayakers.

We arrived at our destination in the late morning and leisurely strolled through Rock City Park. We walked the park's trail bordered with various shapes and sizes of rocks and boulders, some as large as a small house. There were also numerous trails you could choose to walk down. One pathway was bordered with large boulders that were just inches apart; you had to squeeze sideways to get through. We finally made it to the pinnacle of the park, where several states could be seen from one vantage point. We enjoyed the gentle breeze as we sipped beverages and took a rest. We enjoyed the experience and the day together, and it was picture-perfect weather.

On our way home, we decided to drive through the town of Chattanooga. Bob got sick, and I had to pull over in the middle of the road. I think it was due to all the curves as we came down the mountain, but we managed to make it home without further incident.

I had taught Sunday school for several years. Part of my role as teacher involved writing letters to the children in our church. I routinely used the experiences in my life as lessons in these letters, including our trials with cancer. Upon returning from Rock City, I contemplated how those boulders, being several thousand feet above sea level, had been carved and molded by the force of water. How did the water get that high? Were the boulders shaped and then settled in that location after a flood? This was something my mind could only conceive that had happened on a grand scale, and God alone could accomplish that type of feat. So I decided to write the children a letter about our trip.

Dear _____,

Hello! I wonder what you are doing now that you are out of school for summer break. I bet you are planning some great outdoor activities. Speaking of summer activities, my husband and I decided to take a day trip to see Rock City in Chattanooga, Tennessee. Have you ever been there? It's a very beautiful garden of huge rocks and boulders that God created many years ago. You can actually see where the water carved areas into the rocks, and I couldn't help but think that it happened when He flooded the earth back in Noah's time.

In 1923, two missionaries went to Chattanooga to minister to the Indians and discovered this beautiful place. A man and his wife later developed it into a garden. Because they wanted to share it with the world, they made it into a tourist attraction and advertised it all over the country by writing "See Rock City" on people's barns.[35]

The rock garden was very fascinating, and it reminded me of just how awesome God is. I used to live on a river, and I know how water forms and shapes rocks. I thought about the scripture in the Bible in Ephesians 5:25–26, where Jesus says that He loves us (His church, that's *you* and *me!*) and that He gave Himself for us (died on the cross) so that we could be washed from our sins and be made holy by washing us with His Word, the Bible.

I bet you have never thought about Jesus washing you with the words from the Bible. I bet you thought that you could be washed only with soap and water. Just as the stones in the creek, river, or ocean get rounded and smoothed by the water washing over them, so can He wash you and make you holy by the power of His Word. Are you letting Him wash you and make you into a beautiful rock by reading His Word?

Maybe this summer while you are visiting a creek, river, or even the ocean, you could find a beautiful stone or shell that has been shaped and smoothed by the water and put it someplace very special to remind you that Jesus wants to wash you and make you holy by the power of His Word.

Love and in His name,
Kim Doke
ROCKids Teacher

Second Corinthians 4:7–10 reads: "But we have this treasure in earthen vessels, that the excellence of the power may be of God and not of us. We are hard-pressed on every side, yet not crushed; we are perplexed, but not in despair; persecuted, but not forsaken; struck down, but not destroyed—always carrying about in the body the dying of the Lord Jesus, that the life of Jesus also may be manifested in our body."

It was late, and Bob wanted to go downstairs to try to walk off his restless leg syndrome. He had been suffering with it for quite some time. I wanted to go with him, but he insisted he would be fine; he was just going downstairs to walk on our driveway. Most of the residences on our street were overnight vacation rentals or second homes, and we were usually the only people around, with the exception of some apartments a few hundred feet away. I turned on the floodlights and periodically looked over the deck to check on him.

The third time I looked, he was gone. I called, and he didn't answer. I yelled, "Bob?" Still no answer! I became frantic and raced down the stairs, my heart racing as I repeatedly called out his name. Still no answer! It was pitch-dark beyond our front porch, and it took my eyes a few minutes to adjust. I didn't see him anywhere. Frantic and wishing I had a flashlight, I ran under the adjacent cabins, searching and yelling his name. Then it entered my mind that he could have walked into the river's current. I became overwhelmed with fear.

I finally heard a faint, garbled voice calling, "Kim!" I looked up, and Bob was halfway up one of our neighbors' stairs, staggering to hold on to the rail as he turned to respond to my call. He was disoriented and mumbling. I yelled, "Don't move!" then looked towards the apartments and yelled, "Help, help! Please help me," hoping someone would hear. I got up underneath Bob's body to lead him down, taking one step at a time while struggling to hold him up, and we slowly made it back to our cabin.

To get him up our stairs, I positioned myself behind him, grabbed his hip pockets, and pushed him up every step until we reached the top. I led him into the bedroom. He was still disoriented. My nerves frayed and shaking, I shouted, "Did you take something? What did you take?" He had prescriptions for oxycodone, Percocet, and MS Contin (controlled-release morphine), but was only taking Percocet twice a day for pain. Because he had difficulty sleeping, he also had a prescription for Ambien.

I searched the kitchen to see if the pill bottles had been moved, and I saw a small glass on the counter next to a bottle of amaretto. I frantically begged him to tell me what he had taken, knowing I couldn't trust his judgment, but desperate to know if he had overdosed on his pills. He replied but was unable to convey what he had done. I deduced that he had been so desperate to get some sleep he had mixed the amaretto with the Ambien. I couldn't blame him. He was miserable.

I positioned him in bed, and we both lay there for a moment. He was still restless and got up again. After several hours of coaxing and trying to tame his anxiety, I managed to finally get him back into bed, and he fell asleep. It was a night from hell, and thankfully, the next day he didn't remember it.

Bob knew I would most likely remarry one day, and he wanted to make sure I was mortgage free, so he listed our cabin with a realtor. I wanted to be debt free too, but was a little apprehensive at first and wanted to make sure we were doing the right thing. Even though I had made memories in this cabin that would be cherished forever, I had grown weary of the river and its power. I also knew that when he was gone, I would not want to stay there alone. I had witnessed more storms and rising water in the twenty-three months we lived there than I cared to recall, and I was ready to make a change. I loved the experience of living on the river, but the river didn't love me back!

To prepare for a possible sale, I started searching for a nearby rental property that we could move in to once our house was sold. My friend Melodie had a rental cabin just two doors down, also on the river, and her tenant's lease was ending. It was also fully furnished, fulfilling all the comforts of home. We knew, even though it was on the river, that it was the best option available because it was temporary, and Bob was living on bor-rowed time. Each day was a gift, and I lived on the edge always wondering, *Will today be the day?* He continued to lose weight, and his skin color was sallow.

Bob had a buyer who was interested in our cabin, but we couldn't agree on a price. After much contemplating and knowing our situation, he finally made an offer we could work with. Since we sold the house 90 percent furnished, I just needed to move our personal things. That was still a feat for me because I was doing it alone. I also had our office and computer equipment to move and set up. Not an easy job, considering we had fourteen feet of steps at both cabins.

The sale was both pleasant and painful because another chapter of our lives was closing, but it also reminded me that Bob was looking out for me. He was my love, my life, my best friend, and my hero.

CHAPTER 17

The Move Next Door

M y friend Gloria came after work to help me move. I had been going up and down the stairs with boxes all day, and when she arrived, I was tired and wanted to finish moving. Bob walked over to Melodie's to sit outside on the stairs. He enjoyed the river view while watching us go back and forth, wanting to help, but knowing he couldn't. He was feeling fatigued, and Gloria stopped to sit and talk with him for a moment. It was a sweet conversation.

He shared, "I've had a wonderful life. I've had a wonderful marriage with Kim for almost thirty-one years. I've been blessed with great family and friends. I've fought hard, and I'm ready to go. You and Kim have been friends for a long time, and I want you two to come back here, sit on this porch, talk your girl talk, and remember our good times together."

I passed by them as I went back to our cabin, and Gloria got up and followed. When we got to the top of our stairs, I saw tears in her eyes. She told me what Bob had said, and it broke my heart. It was a reminder that the end was approaching, and he was ready. He was already thinking about life after he was gone. Gloria told me she had reassured him that we would definitely get together, have girl talk, and remember that he was the reason why.

We continued our follow-up visits with Bob's oncologist and Dr. Dixon to manage his medicines, labs, and to get his port flushed. Dr. Dixon's report read: "Albumin is 2.5, so things aren't horrible yet. However, I am worried that time may be short. This is discussed with Mr. and Mrs. Doke." He told me Bob could have one week or two months to live.

Ten days later our return visit to Dr. Dixon reported: "His ascites is more significant. He is not having any encephalopathy. She acknowledges he is dying and wants to know more, but I cannot give it at this time without knowing whether we have a trend or whether his liver function is stable. I think he is going downhill now and will talk with him later this week."

Bob's stomach continued to distend, and a CT scan showed the liver was essentially replaced with tumor. He was still taking Aldactone (a diuretic) for edema and ascites, which was still progressing. Dr. Dixon knew our care from this point forward was supportive only. He asked Bob about going into hospice because he knew Bob had previously wanted to be at home when he passed. Dr. Dixon knew how stressful life on the river had been for me and how that affected Bob, and he thought hospice care would be best. We agreed. He asked Bob if he wanted to remain alert or have morphine. Bob's reply was that he wanted enough medication to dull the pain. Dr. Dixon wrote, "Mr. and Mrs. Doke both have a wonderful attitude about his impending death."

Later that day my parents came for a visit. After talking a while, Bob told them, "You were good parents to me, and I really appreciate you."

My dad asked, "What can we do for you, Bob?" and he replied, "Pray for me."

I tried to imagine how Bob felt, but could only try. How would I feel if I knew my days were numbered? My heart ached beyond measure.

Bob began to have a rash that started on the upper part of his chest and ran up his neck behind his ear. It continued to worsen, so we called the doctor and he worked us in. The doctor immediately recognized it as shingles. Bob's system was compromised, so it was not a surprise. The doctor said it was serious because of Bob's condition, and it could go to his brain. If that happened, it would not be good. In addition to the prescription Bob was given, I applied aloe from my plant onto the shingles. They dried up within a few days. We were so excited that we told the doctor so he could tell his other patients.

It was my birthday, and Bob's sister, Cindy, was coming to spend the day. Cindy and her family had recently moved to Cumming, Georgia, and she was so glad to be living near us, especially due to Bob's circumstances. She wanted to learn how to cream corn, so I went to a local farmer's market and purchased a few dozen ears. We spent the day cooking, making fried green tomatoes, and celebrating my birthday. It was a good day, and Bob even managed to eat a few fried green tomatoes.

CHAPTER 18

The Kingdom Nears

≈

Our attorney's wife gave me a book called *Final Gifts: Understanding the Special Awareness, Needs, and Communications of the Dying.* The book was given to me at just the right time because I needed to know more about the final days of Bob's life. I had been so focused on Bob's journey that I hadn't thought much about his end.

The book was written by two hospice nurses and consists of several short stories about their experiences with terminal patients. Through the stories, you learn what a patient may experience before leaving this earth, how they may choose to die when a person is or isn't present, that they may know "today" is the day they are going to die and may call the family to come, and the things they may see, hear, or do that may mean they are getting a glimpse into the spiritual realm.[36] If you have the tools to interpret your loved one's actions in his final days or hours, you can be encouraged rather than discouraged by his transition into the next life, knowing that death is a reality and that it's better to understand than to fight what you can't control.

Proverbs 27:1 says, "Do not boast about tomorrow, for you do not know what a day may bring forth"; and

Isaiah 64:6 says, "We all fade as a leaf." James 4:13–17 expresses the same thought:

> Come now, you who say, 'Today or tomorrow we will go to such and such a city, spend a year there, buy and sell, and make a profit'; whereas you do not know what will happen tomorrow. For what is your life? It is even a vapor that appears for a little time and then vanishes away. Instead you ought to say, 'If the Lord wills, we shall live and do this or that.' But now you boast in your arrogance. All such boasting is evil. Therefore, to him who knows to do good and does not do it, to him it is sin.

None of us know the day or the hour, but just as a season has its signs, we can know our mortality is near. Jesus said in Matthew 24:32–36:

> Now learn this parable from the fig tree: When its branch has already become tender and puts forth leaves, you know that summer is near. So you also, when you see all these things, know that it is near—at the doors! Assuredly, I say to you, this generation will by no means pass away till all these things take place. Heaven and earth will pass away, but My words will by no means pass away. But of that day and hour no one knows, not even the angels of heaven, but My Father only.

"Therefore you also be ready, for the Son of Man is coming at an hour you do not expect" (Matthew 24:44).

You are a triune being—a body, soul, and spirit. Your body goes back to the earth from whence it came, but your spirit lives on. If you choose Jehovah God, who is eternal life, then you will live forever with Him in heaven. If you do not choose Him, then you will live in eternal darkness, separated from this holy God.

He asks, desires, and longs for us to choose Him. He died on a literal cross, being fully God and fully man, taking the full judgment of our sins— past, present, and future—to reconcile us to His Father, the only living God. When we do not choose Him, we leave Him no choice but to condemn us to eternal hell. He paid our penalty with His life to save us from eternal death; the least we can do is honor Him with our lives. If we do, our reward will be an abundant, fulfilled life on this earth, as well as eternal life with Him in heaven.

Because your body and spirit are separate entities, the will of your spirit can help prolong your life. If it wills you to fight, you can live longer. The importance of your will is illustrated in the saying, "Keep your spirits up!" However, sometimes the body wears out before the spirit wants to give up. Bob's spirit was fighting the good fight, but his body had given up. When a body succumbs to death, the spirit has no choice but to leave.

Bob was getting weaker and told the doctor at our next visit, "I'm starting to give up. I don't think Kim will be able to feed me unless it's intravenously." He had just had five liters of fluid drained from his stomach at the hospital. We knew it would give him only temporary relief because it would fill up again. This caused him difficulty in keeping food down, and he had become jaundiced as a result of liver failure.

The next day's forecast predicted another bad storm cell. I contemplated packing up and leaving, but I was tired of running and thought, *If there are no tornado warnings, we can get through it.* The rain began after dinner and continued to worsen. About 7 p.m., a friend called from my church in Cleveland and told me it was storming so badly they couldn't leave. As the storm raged,

I told her I was very worried too but had decided to stay and pray through it; I was not running! She prayed for me over the phone, and then I prayed for her.

At 7:15 p.m., our friend Art called to see if we wanted him to pick us up. I said, "No, we are not running anymore, but thanks!"

He replied, "Okay. Call if you change your mind."

The lightning, wind, and rain became even fiercer. I could not see the river through the sliding glass doors. The lightning was striking every few seconds all around us, vibrating the cabin. Even if I had wanted to leave, I calculated how I would get Bob down the stairs. They were exposed to the elements. For a healthy person, this would be possible, but alarming.

I paced the small cabin, extremely nervous, bolting from room to room as I tried to get a visual on the rising water while boldly praying out loud. Bob was lying on the couch, seemingly oblivious. He had entered into the stage of acceptance and was unaffected by the threatening storm.

Art called again. When he heard the fear in my voice, he said, "We are coming to get you," and I said, "Okay!" When I walked out onto the covered front porch, I couldn't see the driveway under our house; it was a solid body of water several inches deep. The adjacent creek that flowed into the Chattahoochee River had also risen, and the two bodies of water converged under our house, covering the whole area. Our two new cars were parked under the house, and I worried that they could be swept away.

When I saw Art's car lights, we slowly stepped out from under the cover of the porch and began descending the stairs. With umbrella in hand, I went first to lead Bob in order to prevent him from falling. We reached our van, and I opened the passenger side door for Bob to get in first, since I was going to follow Art out. Bob was so worried about his new Volkswagen Bug floating down the river that he turned to go back towards it. We were both soaked, and I yelled, "No, get back in the car!" He persisted but finally waved his hand in defeat. The river had become a sea of whitecaps, flowing with rage.

When leaving our single-lane driveway headed for Art's home in the town of Helen, I realized the bridge and road over the creek were washed out. I had no choice but to turn left. The road ahead split because of a pond on its upper side, and the water had breached its bank, also covering the lower road. I had no choice but to drive on the wrong side of the road to get out. We made it to Art's safely and rode out the storm together—without power. With candles lit, we talked till late evening.

The next day the news in Atlanta reported there were over one thousand lightning strikes recorded in our area in a one-hour period, which averaged one strike every four seconds.[37] That's unrelenting direct strikes for a solid one-hour period! Six inches of rain fell, causing several inches of red mud to cover the concrete driveway beneath our house, and once again we had a mess to clean up. Thankfully, there was a construction crew nearby that had befriended Bob, and they came to help.

Cindy's family went to Florida for a three-day weekend. She knew the storm had taken its toll on me and invited us to stay at her house in Cumming while they were away. It was a welcome relief to get out of the cabin! The weekend was a retreat as we enjoyed the safety and comfort of her home, savoring each day. Bob had a doctor's appointment in Gainesville on Monday, and Cindy and her family returned home Sunday afternoon for her to go to Dr. Dixon's with us.

The next morning we could hardly concentrate on the drive because Bob was sick. He had expelled bile before, but he had been doing it more frequently in the past seven days. He was declining quickly. Once Dr. Dixon saw him, he knew it was time to enter hospice. Northeast Georgia Medical Center had purchased Lanier

Park Hospital, and their hospice floor was in the medical center. Dr. Dixon knew Bob would be more comfortable at Lanier Park, since he had his major surgery there in February and knew most of the nurses, so he arranged the admission.

"Our Father who is in heaven, hallowed be Your name. *Your kingdom come.* Your will be done, on earth as it is in heaven. Give us this day our daily bread. And forgive us our debts, as we also have forgiven our debtors. And do not lead us into temptation, but deliver us from evil. [For *Yours is the kingdom* and the power and the glory forever. Amen.]" (Matthew 6:9–13, NASB, emphasis added).

CHAPTER 19

Hospital Is Home

S ince it was after 5 p.m., Cindy and I had to have Bob admitted to hospice through the emergency room. It pained me to get a wheelchair and make him wait to be admitted. His body was frail, and I knew the chair was uncomfortable, but we had no choice. We were assigned a room, and a transporter came to get us. I asked, "Does Jannie Miller still work here?" Jannie was one of the nurses who had cared for Bob in February. We had grown especially close to her during that hospital stay.

The transporter replied, "Yes, but she's finishing her shift and might be gone."

As we walked down the hallway, I felt so alone. I thought how nice it would be to see her friendly face. I asked, "Can you check to see?"

"Sure!" he replied. The thought of seeing her brought hope and comfort to all of our hearts.

Minutes after we arrived in Bob's room, she came to see us. Bob had just sat on the edge of the bed, and when he saw her peer in the doorway, he beamed. She bolted in, put her arm around his shoulder, and spoke words of comfort. He felt consoled beyond measure, and so did Cindy and I. Throughout our hospital stay, even though Jannie wasn't working Bob's room, she would pop in to say hello.

Bob's blood pressure dropped to 80/40, and his urine was turning dark. He started saying things that didn't make sense. The hospice nurse said that was normal for his condition. I questioned God's timing and why He was allowing Bob to live in this state. I asked Jannie, "Why is he still here?"

Jannie replied, "Because you are blessing us with your strength and spirit in the face of adversity. Don't take that lightly!" I never imagined that the Lord could still be working in the final phase of death. I realized I had not trusted Him when I questioned, and I apologized. Even in the final moments of deep anguish, I knew He had not left us. He was still working on our behalf.

The hospital staff called Bob a miracle man. The next day he wanted a steak dinner, so I went to Longhorn's to pick one up while his mom stayed behind to keep him company. On the drive there, alone and with time to think, I thought about how strange it was that he had rallied and was sitting up and wanting to eat. Later I found out it is not unusual for a person to do this when he is nearing death. It takes you aback at first, and you actually think they are getting better.

Then fear crept into my mind, and I thought, *What if Bob were to die while I'm gone?* I realized, *It would be well with my soul because I know where he is going, and I know I will see him again.* I was reminded of the hymn "It Is Well with My Soul" by Horatio G. Spafford.[38]

Second Corinthians 5:4–7 says, "For we who are in this tent groan, being burdened, not because we want to be unclothed, but further clothed, that *mortality may be swallowed up by life.* Now He who has prepared us for this very thing is God, who also has given us the Spirit as a guarantee. So we are always confident, knowing that while we are at home in the body we are absent from the Lord. For we walk by faith, not by sight" (emphasis added).

My nieces and nephews who lived in Tallahassee drove up on the weekend to see Bob. He slept most of the day, and it was more convenient for them to stay in the lobby until he woke. I rotated back and forth while he slept, visiting with them and checking on him. By early evening, he was finally alert, and they gathered around his bed. It was difficult at first. What do you say? How do you say it? Who will break the silence first?

Bob was the first to speak. He imparted words of wisdom and encouragement to each one. He told Justin he was a fine man. He spoke heartfelt words to Rachel and her fiancé, Trey, about the importance of marriage and his belief in their ability to make it work. He told Emily how proud of her he was. He loved them all dearly. He even made them laugh! Their hearts were heavy and their eyes tearful as they left the room.

After they arrived home, Rachel shared, "While driving home, deep sadness permeated the car. To break the silence I put in a CD by Plankeye. Unbeknownst to me, the song "Goodbye" started playing, and tears started streaming down my face. I looked around and everyone else was crying too. No words were spoken. As we listened to the lyrics, we thought about our visit with Bob—feeling the pain and emotion of having to say good-bye."

After researching the song's lyrics, I realized why it had such an impact on them. The song speaks of life—that we will have rain in it and unfulfilled dreams, that our tree of life will wither one day and we must say farewell. But it will bloom once again! The life we live will leave a legacy, and those left behind will have the memories of it; but even through the pain, the Lord will fill us up.[39] I thought of the scripture that says we must die in order to live (wither, but bloom). When we are beaten down by our trials (pruned), our lives will bloom again as we come out on the other side; and if we pass away, then we will bloom when we get to heaven, receiving the fullness of our sanctification process—a perfected sweet aroma to God!

That Sunday Bob's pain medication was increased. He was getting double morphine with a patch. I called his closest friends to let them know. They meant so much to Bob, and I wanted to give them the opportunity to say good-bye. A few came and stayed for long visits. Bob started to get agitated. He couldn't express his wishes, so he raised his arms in frustration. I quickly realized what was happening and suggested our friends leave so he could get some rest. I felt guilty that I had not guarded his precious time better, but I had made the decision to let others come, and it was too late to change it. I made sure to manage Bob's subsequent visits and keep them short.

Hurricane Katrina had struck New Orleans, and her formidable path was headed for Georgia. I listened to the news and weather all day. Bob was responding very little and slept most of the time. Every county across the southern end of the state was issued a tornado warning. The warnings slowly crept into the northern counties towards us. I wondered, *Is this unforgiving path going to dissipate or continue north, hitting us?* I had seen storms break up before hitting our area, but this one showed no signs of dispersing. It was 9 p.m., and our county hadn't been issued a tornado warning, but it was next to be named. I was very nervous and paced the floor while praying.

The nurse entered, saying, "We need to put Bob's bed into the hallway."

I asked, "Has a tornado warning been issued?"

She responded, "We have orders to prepare by getting all the beds into the hall."

I asked, "Can I help you? It will help take my mind off of being nervous." "Yes!" she replied.

We went down the hall, unlocking beds, moving IV poles, and lining patients down the walls of the hallway. I wanted to hold Bob so much, but he was asleep and unfazed by it all. The warning passed, and we put the patients back into their rooms. The warnings continued northward into our home counties of White and Habersham. My parents and Bob's mom, as well as our cabin, were located laterally in these two counties. I prayed for them as I had prayed for others all day. It was just shy of two weeks since I had been home, and I considered the possibility that Melodie's cabin, along with our things, might be destroyed.

The tornado hit Helen at 12:30 a.m. The rain was fierce. It actually wrapped itself into the tornado, making the tornado invisible. This is called a rain-wrapped tornado. Rain gets sucked into the tornado and is driven horizontally by the winds, making it very dangerous because you cannot see the tornado until it's upon you. The town of Helen was hit hard. There was damage to the post office, the outlet mall, homes, the second floor of a two-story hotel, and the beautiful mountainous terrain surrounding the town and the Chattahoochee River.

Several guests staying at the hotel had escaped the devastation of Katrina by fleeing to Georgia. They beat death once again when the hotel management guided them downstairs right before the top floor was sucked off.

The next morning the phone calls started coming in. No one knew the extent of the damage yet. I asked, "Will you call me as soon as you find out if our cabin was hit?"

Each stated, "Yes! And you are in our thoughts and prayers." Not long after, our friends called to say that a large tree had fallen and landed just a few feet away from our cabin, but that everything was fine.

Later that day more family arrived from Florida. They couldn't get to Melodie's cabin since all roads leading into Helen were open to residents only. Debris and remnants of shredded trees were everywhere. The surrounding forest and landscape were forever changed. It would take decades to grow the trees again. Emergency workers continued to work at clearing the debris to open more roads, and our family was finally able to drive into Helen that afternoon to survey the results firsthand before coming to the hospital.

CHAPTER 20

The Kingdom Cometh!

I was sleeping on a lounge chair next to Bob when he sat straight up and said, "I've gotta go! I've gotta go!" Half-asleep, I thought he needed a bedpan. Then he said, "Don't you hear the whistle?"

It immediately took me back to the book *Final Gifts*. Sometimes when a person is getting ready to die, they see or hear things that are not in this dimension. They may see a relative that has passed, see Jesus, or hear a sound (bell or whistle). Sometimes that sound can relate to their occupation. Caregivers, family, or friends often misinterpret their actions as confused behavior and do not comprehend what their loved one is experiencing. They often respond with, "I don't hear the bell," or "I don't see Aunt Mary [or Jesus]."

These auditory and visual experiences are called "nearing death awareness." This behavior is a nonverbal way of communicating experiences of dying and helps people know they aren't alone, that others who have died are meeting them. I believe God is giving them a glimpse into the dimension they are about to enter. The Bible tells us in David's psalm:

> The Lord is my shepherd, I shall not want. He makes me lie down in green pastures; He leads me beside quiet waters. He restores my soul; He guides me in the paths of righteousness for His name's sake. *Even though I walk through the valley of the shadow of death, I fear no evil,* for You are with me; Your rod and Your staff, they comfort me. You prepare a table before me in the presence of my enemies; You have anointed my head with oil; My cup overflows. Surely goodness and lovingkindness will follow me all the days of my life, And I will dwell in the house of the Lord forever.
>
> —Psalm 23, NASB, emphasis added

You never die when you are a Christian! Just like a shadow passing on a sundial, your spirit passes from this earthly plane to the plane of eternity, and our Father God and Jesus are waiting to greet you there. As Hebrews 12:22–24 explains, "But you have come to Mount Zion and to the city of the living God, the heavenly Jerusalem, and to myriads of angels, to the general assembly and church of the firstborn who are enrolled in heaven, and to God, the Judge of all, and to the spirits of the righteous made perfect, and to Jesus, the mediator of a new covenant, and to the sprinkled blood, which speaks better than the blood of Abel" (NASB). This scripture tells us that not only are God and Jesus there, but also the angels and all those who have gone before us since the beginning of time—Abraham, Moses, David, Paul, and our loved ones. Wow!

We have hope that no other religion can offer or even come close to promising. No other god has entered the very time and space that He created, has been born of a virgin, died on a cross, resurrected from a grave, and given mankind a Holy Spirit, other than the living God

Jehovah, the God of the universe and the Bible. And no other god has had over five hundred witnesses testifying about His resurrection (read 1 Corinthians 15:1–8). As 1 Timothy 6:15–16 reminds us, "He who is the blessed and only Sovereign, the King of kings and Lord of lords, who alone possesses immortality and dwells in unapproachable light, whom no man has seen or can see. To Him be honor and eternal dominion! Amen" (NASB).

Then there are the countless lives that this gospel, the gospel of Jesus Christ, has changed, never to be the same again. Bob knew where he was going, and God had given him the peace to walk through that valley. It was only a valley of a shadow, not death itself! Bob knew his life was only shifting from one plane to another in order to spend eternity with our Lord.

The next day I called Cindy and asked if she could come to the hospital to stay with us. Bob's breathing had become labored, and the day had been difficult. When Dr. Dixon came in that evening, he took me into the hall and said with sadness, "I think it's time for morphine under the tongue. Are you all right with that?"

Tearing up, I said, "Yes, I knew this time was coming." He affirmatively nodded, and we hugged. When I told Cindy what he had said, we were both glad she had come. I called our families to let them know that Bob's time was nearing.

That night tears flooded my pillow as I thought about our trial, the good fight Bob had fought, our lives, the fact that this was it. The end was not near—it was here. Bob would be gone forever. My companion, who had always called me "his bride" even after thirty years of marriage, would cease to exist in this physical realm. I was so thankful for the time God had given me Bob, extending his life seventeen months past the time frame given by the doctors. A young woman from my church had recently died while reaching for her inhaler during an asthma attack. She was on her way to a mortgage closing after picking her son up from school. I recall thinking that not only is your next day not promised, but also not even your next breath.

Cindy and I woke at 7:20 the next morning from Bob's heightened agitation and labored breathing. The hospice nurses came in and began to monitor his vitals. Never having experienced death before, I was walking in unfamiliar territory. Even though I had read the book *Final Gifts*, I did not know how Bob's individual death process would play out, nor did I know how I would handle it. I was trying to be strong, but I felt numb at times.

After receiving my phone call, my brother's family, after just returning to Tallahassee a few days prior, jumped back into the car to return to the hospital. They arrived early that morning, and we all gathered around Bob's bed in a horseshoe shape, some leaning in to talk to him, some just staring, another walking the hall to escape witnessing the inevitable.

I had already given Bob permission to leave this world. Giving permission is sometimes necessary to do, and I didn't understand why it was taking so long. I thought his death would be quick, and I hadn't anticipated how lengthy the process of his body shutting down would be. I wondered, *Why can't he just slip away peacefully?* I recalled a story in *Final Gifts* of how a patient had waited until his wife left the room to pass. It dawned on me that perhaps Bob was not dying because I was there. With all my family around him, I walked out into the hall, hoping for finality.

Nothing changed, and his labored breathing continued. Then Cindy came to get me, saying, "Kim, the nurse says it's going to be soon."

I bolted to Bob's bed, cradled his head in my arms, caressed his cheek, and whispered into his ear, "It's okay to leave." He took one last breath, his spirit simultaneously departed, and his face instantly grew cold. I didn't hesitate; I removed myself from his bed and pulled the sheet over his face. As 2 Corinthians 5:8 says, "We are confident, yes, well pleased rather to be absent from the body and to be present with the Lord."

The hospice nurse had told me that when he passed, "You can stay in the room with him as long as you like." At the time, I had no idea how I would handle it, but my reaction to his passing proved my faith and belief that Bob was finally home. I thought, *God, You have given me this beloved man for almost thirty-one years. He has just left and is now in Your presence. I do not need to lie with a body that has no spirit.*

I had peace about Bob's passing, that his fight was finally over, and my faith was reaffirmed. I did not know where I would go or what I would do next, but I was at peace. "Peace I leave with you, My peace I give to you; not as the world gives do I give to you. Let not your heart be troubled, neither let it be afraid. You have heard Me say to you, 'I am going away and coming back to you.' If you loved Me, you would rejoice because I said, 'I am going to the Father,' for My Father is greater than I" (John 14:27–28).

Bob's sanctification process was now consummated. He had come to the end of his life on earth and was now perfected in heaven with Christ. The *Ryrie Study Bible* gives a good explanation of the process of salvation and sanctification. It can be viewed in three aspects in the New Testament as the three Ps of sanctification: *positional, progressive,* and *perfected.* Positional is the moment of your salvation when you accept the gospel of Jesus Christ and are set apart to God (1 Corinthians 6:11); progressive is the act of living out your life in holiness as you walk by faith, letting Him take you from faith to glory (1 Thessalonians 4:3–8); and perfected is when you enter heaven and receive your glorified body perfected in Christ Jesus (1 Thessalonians 3:13 and Phillipians 3:20–21).[40]

Bob entered heaven at 10:40 a.m. on Thursday, September 1, 2005. He lived on earth for fifty-two years. This date would be one I would never forget, along with his celebration of life, his funeral. It was on Labor Day weekend. What a time to be birthed into the kingdom of heaven! He was birthed into this world through his mother's natural labor and was birthed into the kingdom of God through spiritual labor. As Job 19:25–27 says, "For I know that my Redeemer lives, and He shall stand at last on the earth; and after my skin is destroyed, this I know, that in my flesh I shall see God, whom I shall see for myself, and my eyes shall behold, and not another."

In the early church, the term *birthdays* was applied to the festivals of martyrs, the days on which they suffered death in this world and were born to the glory and life of heaven.[41] What a glorious truth to know, that birthdays have a deeper meaning!

Psalm 139:13–18 declares:

> For You formed my inward parts; You covered me in my mother's womb. I will praise You, for I am fearfully and wonderfully made; marvelous are Your works, and that my soul knows very well. My frame was not hidden from You, when I was made in secret, and skillfully wrought in the lowest parts of the earth. Your eyes saw my substance, being yet unformed. And in Your book they all were written, the days fashioned for me, when as yet there were none of them.
>
> How precious also are Your thoughts to me, O God! How great is the sum of them! If I should count them, they would be more in number than the sand; when I awake, I am still with You.

Oh death, where is your sting? There is no sting!

Now this I say, brethren, that flesh and blood cannot inherit the kingdom of God; nor does corruption inherit incorruption. Behold, I tell you a mystery: We shall not all sleep, but we shall all be changed—in a moment, in the twinkling of an eye, at the last trumpet. For the trumpet will sound, and the dead will be raised incorruptible, and we shall be changed. For this corruptible must put on incorruption, and this mortal must put on immortality. So when this corruptible has put on incorruption, and this mortal has put on immortality, then shall be brought to pass the saying that is written: "Death is swallowed up in victory. O Death, where is your sting? O Hades, where is your victory?" The sting of death is sin, and the strength of sin is the law. But thanks be to God, who gives us the victory through our Lord Jesus Christ.

—1 Corinthians 15:50–57

There was no sting in death for Bob, nor will there be for me. We have victory because death has been defeated by Christ's victory over our sins. There is no eternal death for anyone who chooses Him, only death of the physical body. "Therefore there is now no condemnation for those who are in Christ Jesus. For the law of the Spirit of life in Christ Jesus has set you free from the law of sin and of death" (Romans 8:1–2, NASB).

Bob had hope! I, and all who believe, have hope! And hope does not disappoint. First Peter 1:3–9 expresses it clearly:

Blessed be the God and Father of our Lord Jesus Christ, who according to His abundant mercy has begotten us again to a living hope through the resurrection of Jesus Christ from the dead, to an inheritance incorruptible and undefiled and that does not fade away, reserved in heaven for you, who are kept by the power of God through faith for salvation ready to be revealed in the last time. In this you greatly rejoice, though now for a little while, if need be, you have been grieved by various trials, that the genuineness of your faith, being much more precious than gold that perishes, though it is tested by fire, may be found to praise, honor, and glory at the revelation of Jesus Christ, whom having not seen you love. Though now you do not see Him, yet believing, you rejoice with joy inexpressible and full of glory, receiving the end of your faith—the salvation of your souls.

Jesus is returning! Bob will be raised to join Him first, and if I'm still alive on the earth, then will I. First Thessalonians 4:14–17 says:

For if we believe that Jesus died and rose again, even so God will bring with Him those who sleep in Jesus [those who have already died].
For this we say to you by the word of the Lord, that we who are alive and remain until the coming of the Lord will by no means precede those who are asleep. For the Lord Himself will descend from heaven with a shout, with the voice of an archangel, and

with the trumpet of God. And the dead in Christ will rise first. Then we who are alive and remain shall be caught up together with them in the clouds to meet the Lord in the air. And thus we shall always be with the Lord.

CHAPTER 21

Remembrances

❧

The funeral home director, Brian Alexander, arrived at the hospital, and we went into a side room to discuss the details of the funeral. Even though Bob and I, along with our parents, had made funeral arrangements together, there were still many details to be worked out. What clothing would Bob wear? What items should we put near the casket to represent his life—pictures, locksmith memorabilia?

Since it was a holiday weekend, we knew a lot of people would be out of town, but I didn't want to postpone his funeral another week. So we scheduled the memorial service for Friday evening at six and the funeral on Saturday at two in the afternoon. It all seemed so quick! When we finished, everyone disbanded and left the hospital. I suddenly realized I was alone. This was it. It was final.

On my way out of the hospital, I walked past Bob's room one more time, wondering if I should go in, then thought, *I don't need to see him again. I know his body is just a shell without a spirit—his spirit is gone!* Numb and emotionless, I walked to my van and sat inside, staring out the window. I stared for a long while, wanting to cry but not able to. I regained composure. Tears welled up as I searched for my list to make phone calls to inform friends of Bob's passing. I grappled to finish calling. Then I drove back to the cabin in Helen. The drive home was the loneliest I've ever had. I pondered how the book of our lives had been written, and the last chapter was completed. Now a new book would be written, but without Bob.

I picked out Bob's locksmith shirt, pants, and my favorite picture showing his infectious smile and took them to the funeral home. Brian and I took care of business, and then we had a long talk. He was a good friend of Bob's, and he had many fond memories with him. I knew it would be hard for Brian to prepare Bob's body, but he persevered. His professionalism never wavered.

To encourage Brian to prepare for this difficult task, I talked about embalming in the Bible and how spices and ointment were wrapped around the body with strips of linen cloth. He nodded affirmatively. "Preparing the body for burial is necessary," I said, and I was thankful that God had given Brian the gift to be able to prepare Bob's body.

I asked Brian, "Why do you think Bob died the way he did? Why didn't he die quickly instead of having labored breathing while his organs shut down one by one?"

He lovingly replied, "Bob's fight showed that he loved life and didn't want to give up. His spirit fought till it couldn't fight anymore." He continued, "In my profession, I can tell a lot about a person—your organs reveal a lot about you. If you are a bitter person inside, it shows; and Bob was a very happy person!"

The Bible says that what comes out of a man is what defiles him—out of his heart. Matthew 23:27 says, "For you are like whitewashed tombs which on the outside appear beautiful, but inside they are full of dead men's bones and all uncleanness" (NASB). What a vessel (body) has taken in will eventually come out. If a vessel is filled with good things, it will show not only on the outside, but also on the inside. It made perfect sense why Bob died the way he did—holding on. We were so in love—soul mates—and Bob had clung to life until he couldn't fight anymore, holding on until he knew my security was ensured. He had spoken with family members about my care even while fighting for his life.

I returned to the funeral home early Friday evening to make sure everything was in order. Brian privately took me in to see Bob's body. He had positioned his mouth with a perfect little smile. It was as if Bob were alive, and I could imagine a little gleam in his eye. It was just right! Bob's personality was reflected, even in death.

Visitors began to arrive, and before I knew it, three hours had passed. I stood at the head of the casket, with the guests forming a line the length of the room that continued out the door into the hallway. I was filled with an energy I hadn't anticipated. I kept telling people, "I feel so blessed!" I'm sure observers wondered how I could stand there with such fullness of heart. It was because of the gratitude I felt for all God had done in our lives and for the years He had given me with Bob.

Jeremiah 17:7–8 says, "Blessed is the man who trusts in the Lord, and whose hope is the Lord. For he shall be like a tree planted by the waters, which spreads out its roots by the river, and will not fear when heat comes; but its leaf will be green, and will not be anxious in the year of drought, nor will cease from yielding fruit." This scripture epitomized how I felt; I could yield fruit in my year of drought simply because my faith was in the Lord.

The next morning we gathered at the funeral home to organize the details of the procession. Bob's hearse was unique, and special arrangements had to be made for it. One of his customers had been the Antique Auto and Buggy Museum in Helen, Georgia. One day while servicing this customer, he saw an early 1900s antique horse-drawn hearse. This shiny black carriage-style hearse would have been custom-made for a dignitary during the turn of the century. It was adorned with two brass lanterns mounted on each side. The hearse was made of glass side panels that displayed two brass candelabras inside. In their day, these candelabras represented the drape of flowers we now use. Bob quipped, "When I die, I want to be taken out in this!"

Doug, the owner, laughed and said, "Sure!" Bob never would have guessed then that his wish would be fulfilled.

Bob's funeral paid homage to his life. Part of his service included an interpretive dance to the song "I Can Only Imagine" by Mercy Me. I included this in the service because I wanted those attending to be reminded of being in God's presence. Bob's funeral songs would not be stale dirges, but ones to reflect, encourage, enliven, embrace, give hope, and fulfill the soul.

Bob's casket exited the memorial service with Louis Armstrong's "What a Wonderful World." It was a reminder that Bob had loved life and people with all his heart, and he wanted them to laugh, love, and enjoy life and other people. That song embodied all that he was.

When the horse-drawn hearse left the church and entered Highway 129 to make its way through Cleveland, vehicles pulled over on both sides of the road. I was in a limousine right behind Bob's hearse, and I couldn't help but watch the progression of people's faces as heads turned, mouths dropped, and they mouthed words of exclamation. Two ash-white horses pulled the coach. Their manes and tales, elegantly braided, flapped gracefully as the horses made the two-and-a-half-mile journey to the cemetery south of town for the graveside ceremony.

Cranley drove his B & T Lock & Key service van directly behind me. His back window had an oval-shaped decal to memorialize Bob's life. It read "John 3:16, In Memory of Bob Doke, 1953–2005, WWJD." He too had witnessed God's sanctifying work in Bob's life and was touched by Bob's journey. He wanted to honor Bob, but more so, to honor the Lord. Cranley continues to keep

Bob's business alive, and occasionally I still see him driving his van. Today the business is in its twenty-first year of serving the north Georgia area.

Not long after Bob was diagnosed, we visited the cemetery with our parents, pondering the decisions we would be making. We decided to move our graves from one side of the cemetery to the other. Originally our graves required a flat memorial plate for the grave marker, but this side of the cemetery required an upright marker. I had studied and written curriculum on the ancient Hebrew blood covenant and had a new understanding of what a memorial marker meant.

The blood-covenant ceremony entails nine steps. There are three different situations when the blood-covenant ceremony has been performed: in the Old Testament, with the blood of Jesus Christ, and in marriage. In one of the covenant steps, a memorial was established to testify to the covenant that had been entered into. This memorial could be a tree that was planted or a heap of stones that was set up as a reminder of the covenant. A tamarisk tree was often used, which is long lasting, has hard wood, and has evergreen leaves. This represented the enduring grace of the faithful, covenant-keeping God. In the Old Testament, God made a unilateral covenant with Abram (Genesis 12:1-9, 13:14-18, 15:1-21, 17:1-27, 22:1-19. This covenant was for land (Israel), seed (Jesus Christ), and blessing (to all who would receive Him.)

As I studied, I realized just how much God is a covenant-keeping God. He gave us His memorials—His written Word, the Bible; the virgin birth; the cross; the resurrection; His Holy Spirit, and Communion. Just as a memorial stands for something that has happened, these are God's covenant memorials for all to see. His testament—His testimony!

As I thought about the significance of memorializing an event, it occurred to me that Bob deserved a memorial to celebrate his time on earth because of the sanctifying work the Lord had done in his life. We had never wanted to spend a great deal of money on our graves or funerals, but this information gave me new meaning for the remembrance of a life lived.

After Bob died, I walked around other cemeteries to get ideas for his headstone and finally came across one that said, "He lived to ride and rode to live!" I knew this person loved to ride motorcycles. Taking that inspiration, I wrote what Bob meant to those he met. I placed a granite bench opposite his headstone that read, "A man who loved life and people with all his heart and who always left you with a smile." On one side of his headstone are the usual life and death dates and his portrait in porcelain, and the other side is inscribed with: "Rise up, my love, my fair one, and come away. For lo, the winter is past, the rain is over and gone. The flowers appear on the earth; the time of singing has come" (Song of Solomon 2:10–12). This scripture reminded me that Bob's pain and suffering were over, and he was now basking in the beauty and joy of God's presence in heaven.

Second Corinthians 4:16–18 says, "Therefore we do not lose heart. Even though our outward man is perishing, yet the inward man is being renewed day by day. For our light affliction, which is but for a moment, is working for us a far more exceeding and eternal weight of glory, while we do not look at the things which are seen, but at the things which are not seen. For the things which are seen are temporary, but the things which are not seen are eternal."

After Bob's funeral, I wrote a letter of gratitude that was published in our local newspaper. In it, I thanked his doctors, nurses, hospice staff, friends, and family for playing a part in Bob's life and making his time on earth special. Vivian, a local businesswoman I had become friends with through our shared love of the Lord, saw my letter and clipped it out of the paper. She was excited to see it and wanted to mail it to me; but after taping it on her fridge, she couldn't bring herself to part with it. After a year had passed, she was ready to take it down and send it to me. Along with the article, she enclosed a sweet note saying, "Bob's eyes smiled at me every time I looked at it, and I couldn't part with it until now. I'm giving him back to you."

Turn-of-the-century horse-drawn hearse

Company van with dings, dents, and Bob's memorial

**Family picture at Bob's funeral. Someone said
"Give me a Bob Doke smile!"**

Bob's Family

CHAPTER 22

Words of Wisdom

Throughout our whole twenty-three-month trial, the Lord granted us His immeasurable mercy. God's timing was perfect, allowing Bob to draw his last breath at the preordained moment and pass from this plane into God's. During our trial, I discovered that most people are not equipped for dealing with a person who is fighting a terminal disease or with someone experiencing a loss.

After Bob passed, it was common for me to hear, "Oh, he's in heaven now," or "He's not suffering any longer," while sincerely patting me on the shoulder. Even though I knew it, my heart and soul were pierced every time I heard it. I knew he was in heaven, but my soul (mind, will, emotions) was separated from him, and I was grieving.

The Bible describes the marriage relationship as two being one in spirit. Half of me was gone, and I was mourning the loss. Even though I didn't go through the five stages of grief when Bob was diagnosed or while fighting for his life, I had to grieve his loss and my former life. Even in the pain, I knew God was bearing my burden and that I would come through on the other side; I just didn't know when.

The Lord sent the Holy Spirit to console my broken heart, and He sent dear family members and friends to minister to me. Some recognized that I didn't need to hear things I already knew. Instead, they let me talk about my grief and listened to me tell stories about Bob, which was a way of keeping his spirit alive. Others told me they knew it was hard and they were praying for me. As a grieving widow, that was the best support I needed.

Trials and grief are unique to each person, and even though you may have experienced similar circumstances, it's best to not give advice, unless it is godly advice, and even then you must walk sensitively. Nor should you tell someone you know how they feel. Their experiences are unique to them. It's best to console them. You may share how you suffered, but be brief; and most of all, be supportive by listening.

When you understand that grief is part of the process of healing, the wisdom of consoling and how to navigate through it will give greater comfort to both you and the recipient. Before you console, consider the recipient's circumstances, their relationship to the deceased, their spiritual maturity, and any other variables that might affect their journey of grieving.

I thank the Lord for the precious time He granted Bob and me. Judy Garland once said, "For it was not into my ear you whispered, but into my heart. It was not my lips you kissed, but my soul."[42] Bob whispered into my heart and kissed my soul, and I will forever be grateful for his love, friendship, dedication, and sacrifices, as well as his tenacity during his trial. He is my hero and inspiration.

I pray that my story gives you hope and encouragement to persevere in your trial. I pray it inspires and draws you to find the one true lover of your soul, Jesus Christ—the only one who can give you peace, true peace, in any situation you find yourself in.

"Set me as a seal upon your heart, as a seal upon your arm; for love is as strong as death. . . . Many waters cannot quench love, nor can the floods drown it" (Song of Solomon 8:6, 7). God's love for His children is as strong as death. His Son proved it by dying on a cross. He is the way to God the Father. "For by grace you have been saved through faith, and that not of yourselves; it is the gift of God, not of works, lest anyone should boast" (Ephesians 2:8–9).

Isaiah 61 states that He, and only He, can give you the garment of salvation, cover you with a robe of righteousness, give you beauty for ashes, lift your spirit of despair with a garment of praise, heal your broken heart, and give you the oil of joy instead of mourning so that you may be called a tree of righteousness, planted by the Lord to display His splendor that He may be glorified. Let death be a reminder that our life on earth fades like the flower, but God's Word stands forever.

In God's book, endings are always the prelude to new beginnings. Part of the beauty of every sunset is that it gives us hope for a new day. The people of Hawaii must understand well that good-byes and hellos, endings and beginnings, are not opposites. Instead, they are complements to each other, engaging in a symbiotic relationship. In Hawaii, the word *aloha* is used as a greeting to say hello and as a way to bid farewell, or say good-bye. In addition, *aloha* means love and affection, the kind that doesn't just come and go, but endures through all our hellos and good-byes.[43]

So I close with *aloha*! May you find love that endures through your hellos, good-byes, losses, and tears. May this love carry you forward towards your dreams and your future. Aloha!

In the spirit of Bob, who always left you with a joke:

"What did the coffin say when it fell off the hearse?"
"Let's rehearse it!"

Kim's Favorite Quotes

These quotes, along with the scriptures mentioned in this book, helped me through the valley and beyond.

1. Vivian Greene: "Life is not about waiting for the storms to pass. . . . It's about learning how to dance in the rain."[44]

2. Randy Armstrong: "Worrying does not take away tomorrow's troubles. It takes away today's peace."[45]

3. Winston Churchill: "Never, never, never give up."[46] (This was one of Bob's favorites)

4. Haitian proverb: "Beyond the mountains there are mountains again."[47]

5. Chinese proverb: "No matter how tall the mountain, it cannot block out the sun."[48]

6. Peter Benson: "It's better to light a candle than to curse the darkness."[49]

7. Corrie ten Boom: "No pit is so deep that He is not deeper still."[50]

8. Helen Keller: "What we have once enjoyed and deeply loved we can never lose, for all that we love deeply becomes a part of us."[51]

9. An Irish headstone: "Death leaves a heartache no one can heal, love leaves a memory no one can steal."[52]

10. William Shakespeare Othell: "What wound did ever heal but by degrees."[53]

11. John Wesley: "Do all the good you can. By all the means you can. In all the ways you can. In all the places you can. At all the times you can. To all the people you can. As long as you ever can."[54]

12. Mark Twain: "Twenty years from now you will be more disappointed by the things that you didn't do than by the ones you did do. So throw off the bowlines. Sail away from the safe harbor. Catch the trade winds in your sails. Explore. Dream. Discover."[55]

13. Saint Francis of Assisi: "For it is in giving that we receive."[56]

14. Corrie ten Boom: "Never be afraid to trust an unknown future to trust a known God."[57]

15. Ecclesiastes 3:11: "He has made everything beautiful in its time. Also He has put eternity in their hearts, except that no one can find out the work that God does from beginning to end."

16. Elizabeth George: "Take joy home, and make a place in thy great heart for her, and give her time to grow, and cherish her! Then will she come and often sing to thee."[58]

17. Benjamin Malachi Franklin: "The Weaver"

My life is but a weaving
Between my Lord and me;
I cannot choose the colors
He worketh steadily.

Oft times He weaveth sorrow
And I, in foolish pride,
Forget He sees the upper,
And I the underside.

Not till the loom is silent
And the shuttles cease to fly,
Shall God unroll the canvas
And explain the reason why.

The dark threads are as needful
In the Weaver's skillful hand,
As the threads of gold and silver
In the pattern He has planned.[59]

I Can Dance Once Again
By Kim Doke Fletter
December 17, 2007
(This poem was written while going through the
grieving process.)

"You can do it, you can do it, I know you can.
I've got a plan, you're in My hand, yes you can!"

"But it's so lonely, oh so lonely, are you sure I can?"
"Yes you can, yes you can, YES, you can!"

He's been there so many times nudging,
"Look what you've done not begrudging,
Living life for My kingdom and Me,
You know I love you, can't you see?
I'm not leaving, My word says so—it must be!"

"Yes, I can do all things through Christ,
who strengthens me,
He's the one, He's the one, He did it before,
He'll do it again, just like then, yes,
He'll do it just like before!"

He's faithful, oh so faithful, saying,
"Yes, you can get through this, yes you can!
It's only a valley where mountains connect,
Where wisdom and knowledge gained will later
command respect."

I once responded,
"I'm hanging in there, yes, I'm hanging in,"
But it's only because of Christ's death
That I can pursue with excellence!

His words echo, "Yes, you can do it, you can do it,
You can dance once again!"
"Yes, I can dance, I can dance again,
And pursue
Because of His excellence!"

Xulon Press

"Xulon is an ancient Greek word found in the Bible. John the Apostle uses the word xulon to describe the Book of Life and the Tree of Life in Revelation 22:19. Xulon is pronounced 'Zoo-lon.' At Xulon Press, our mission is to add names to God's Book of Life through the books that we publish."[60]

My prayer is that your name is added
to God's Book of Life too!

Kim Doke Fletter

References

1. "Fran Tarkenton," Pro Football Hall of Fame, accessed November 26, 2013, http://www.profootballhof.com/hof/member.aspx?PLAYER_ID=209.

2. "Cancer Staging Fact Sheet," National Cancer Institute, accessed November 26, 2013, http://www.cancer.gov/cancertopics/factsheet/detection/staging.

3. "Stomach (Gastric) Cancer Prevention (PDQ®)," National Cancer Institute, accessed November 26, 2013, http://www.cancer.gov/cancertopics/pdq/prevention/gastric/HealthProfessional.

4. "LMS Research, Houston, Texas," Cynthia Solomon Holmes Foundation, accessed November 27, 2013, http://curelms.webs.com/what-is-leiomyosarcoma.

5. "NCI Dictionary of Cancer Terms," s.v. "C-kit," Cancer.gov, accessed November 27, 2013, http://www.cancer.gov/dictionary?cdrid=44329.

6. Chandalyn Williams, "About Us," Cynthia Solomon Holmes Foundation, accessed January 29, 2014, https://www.thedriven.net/the-cynthia-solomon-holmes-foundation/about-us.

7. Ibid.

8. doctordee, "LeioMyoSarcoma LMS Is a Rare Cancer," *What is Leiomyosarcoma?*, accessed October 23, 2003, www.leiomyosarcoma.org/basic.htm.

9. Wikipedia Contributors, s.v. "Carl Sandburg," *Wikipedia the Free Encyclopedia*, accessed January 29, 2014, http://en.wikipedia.org/wiki/Carl_Sandburg.

10. National Cancer Institute, "Advanced Cancer Living Each Day," (Bethesda, MD: National Cancer Institute, 1998), 32–33.

11. "M. D. Anderson Again Named Nation's Top Cancer Hospital," MDAnderson.org, accessed May 13, 2014, http://www.mdanderson.org/newsroom/news-releases/2004/07-02-04-m-d-anderson-again-named-nation-s-top-cancer-hospital.html.

12. "The Cancer Cell," CancerResearchUK.org, accessed January 29, 2014, http://www.cancerresearchuk.org/cancer-help/about-cancer/what-is-cancer/cells/the-cancer-cell.

    "When Cell Communication Goes Wrong," Learn.Genetics.Utah.edu, accessed January 29, 2014, http://learn.genetics.utah.edu/content/begin/cells/badcom/.

13. National Cancer Institute, "Chemotherapy and You, a Guide to Self-Help During Cancer Treatment," (National Cancer Institute, n.d.), 15–17.

14. Rocky Scott, "Cancer-Fighting 'Future' Here," *Tallahassee Democrat* (Tallahassee, FL), December 12, 2003.

15. "Clinical Trials FAQ," Georgia Cancer Specialists, accessed October 23, 2003, www.gacancer.com/ clinical_trials/index.html.

16. "About the Park," USSAlabama.com, accessed January 29, 2014, http://www.ussalabama.com/ about_park.php.

    "50 Fun Facts," USSAlabama.com, accessed January 29, 2014, http://www.ussalabama.com/ fun_facts.php.

    "Battleship USS Alabama," USSAlabama.com, accessed January 29, 2014, http://www.ussala-bama.com/.

17. Crescentcitybeignets.com., accessed January 29, 2014, http://www.crescentcitybeignets.com/ beignet.html.

    "What is the Origin of Beignets? How the Beignet immigrated to America," Ehow.com, accessed May, 13, 2014, http://www.ehow.com/about_5329694_ origin-beignets.html.

18. Wikipedia Contributors, s.v. "Reliant Astrodome," *Wikipedia the Free Encyclopedia,* accessed January 29, 2014, http://en.wikipedia.org/wiki/ Houston_Astrodome.

19. Selah, *You Raise Me Up* accessed March 13, 2014, http://www.lyricsmania.com/you_raise_me_up_ lyrics_selah.html.

20. "GIST Support International—Gleevec (imatinib mesylate)," GIST Support International, accessed November 22, 2013, http://www.gistsupport.org/treatments-for-gist/gleevec.php.

    doctordee, "Leiomyosarcoma LMS Is a Rare Cancer," Treatment Option Overview, STI-571 (Glivec), accessed October 23, 2003, www.leiomyosarcoma.org/basic.htm.

21. "Aquarium Restaurant—Kemah, TX," Aquarium Restaurants, accessed January 30, 2014, http://www.aquariumrestaurants.com/aquariumkemah/dining.asp.

22. Rita Elkin, *Limu Moui Prize Sea Plant of the South Pacific,* (Woodland Publishing, 2001), quoted in www.Robertas.biz, accessed January 30, 2014, http://www.robertas.biz/media/whatislimu.pdf.

23. Wikipedia Contributors, s.v. "Port (medical)," *Wikipedia the Free Encyclopedia,* accessed January 30, 2014, http://en.wikipedia.org/wiki/Port_(medical).

24. "Scientific Validation for Glyconutrients," Glyconutrientsreference.com, accessed May 13, 2014, http://www.glyconutrientsreference.com/whatareglyconutrients/scientificvalidation.php.

25. "A User's Guide," Physicians' Desk Reference for Nonprescription Drugs and Dietary Supplements, Manntech, 2002.

26. Ray Gebauer, e-mail message to Marcia Moore, "Marcia, What Is the Big Deal about Ambrotose?" April 8, 2003.

27. Maggie Callanan and Patricia Kelley, *Final Gifts: Understanding the Special Awareness, Needs, and Communications of the Dying* (New York: Bantam Books, 1997), 38.

28. "Facts about Niagara Falls," *NiagaraFallsLive.com,* accessed January 30, 2014, http://www.niagara-fallslive.com/Facts_about_Niagara_Falls.htm.

    "Niagara Falls State Park" NiagaraFallsStatePark.com, accessed January 30, 2014, www.niagara-fallsstatepark.com/.

29. "What Is a PICC Line and Why Do I Need It?" *PiccLineNursing.com,* accessed January 30, 2014, http://picclinenursing.com/picc_why.html.

30. "Hurricane Ivan, 2004: Reports, Photos, and Links," 2004Hurricanes.com, accessed January 30, 2014, http://www.2004hurricanes.com/ivan.html.

31. "Gettysburg National Military Park," U.S. National Park Service, accessed January 30, 2014, http://www.nps.gov/gett/index.htm.

    "History & Culture— Gettysburg National Military Park," U.S. National Park Service, accessed January 30, 2014, http://www.nps.gov/gett/historyculture/index.htm.

32. *TheFreeDictionary,* s.v, "Arteriogram," accessed January 30, 2014, http://medical-dictionary.the-freedictionary.com/arteriogram.

33. "Patient Education Brochure SIR Spheres™," SIRTeX Medical, accessed November 4, 2004, http://www.sirtex.com/?p=303.

"Q & A for Patients Brochure," SIRTeX Medical, accessed November 4, 2004, http://www.sirtex.com/?p=303.

34. "Variceal Bleeding Management Procedures," The Cleveland Clinic, accessed March 20, 2005. http://www.clevelandclinic.org/health/health-info/docs/1900/1930.

35. "Our Story: The History of Rock City Gardens," SeeRockCity.com, accessed December 5, 2013, http://seerockcity.com/pages/Our-Story/.

36. Maggie Callanan and Patricia Kelley, *Final Gifts: Understanding the Special Awareness, Needs, and Communications of the Dying* (New York: Bantam Books, 1997), 173.

37. Gene Norman, Certified Broadcast Meteorologist™, Atlanta (CBS *46 News*), e-mail message to Dorothy Kinsey, August 25, 2005.

38. Horatio G. Spafford, *It Is Well with My Soul*, 1873, accessed March 13, 2014, http://library.timelesstruths.org/music/It_Is_Well_with_My_Soul/.

39. Plankeye,*Goodbye*, accessed March 13, 2014, http://www.lyricsmania.com/goodbye_lyrics_plankeye.html.

40. Charles C. Ryrie, ed., "Notes on 1 Thessalonians 4:3," In *Ryrie Study Bible*, expanded ed., NASB, 1995, p. 1908.

41. Merrill F. Unger et al, *The New Unger's Bible Dictionary* (Chicago: Moody Press, 1988), 173.

42. Judy Garland, "For it was not into my ear you whispered, but into my heart. It was not my lips you...," BrainyQuote.com, accessed May 13, 2014, http://www.brainyquote.com/quotes/quotes/j/judygarlan100718.

43. Rev. Kenneth C. Haugk, Ph.D., *Journeying through Grief*, book 4 (St. Louis: Stephen Ministries, 2004), 39.

44. Vivian Green, GoodReads.com, accessed May 13, 2014, https://www.goodreads.com/quotes/386763-life-is-not-about-waiting-for-the-storms-to-pass.

45. Randy Armstrong, "Worrying does not take away tomorrow's troubles...," GoodReads.com, accessed January 21, 2014, http://www.goodreads.com/quotes/612549-worrying-does-not-take-away-to-morrow-s-troubles-it-takes-away.

46. Winston Churchill, "Never, never, never give up," GoodReads.com, accessed January 21, 2014, https://www.goodreads.com/author/quotes/2834066.Winston_Churchill.

47. Haitian Proverb, "Beyond the mountains there are mountains again," Tribe.net, accessed January 21, 2014, http://people.tribe.net/d1b3f2fc-da32-45ac-813c-03b1c3dd0d97/photos/0c3c94bb-1e7c-4e63-8425-f4d7bfbaa821.

48. Chinese proverbs and Chinese sayings, "No matter how tall the mountain, it cannot block out the sun," Chinese-Sayings.com, accessed January 21, 2014, http://

chinese-sayings.com/no-matter-how-tall-the-mountain-it-cannot-block-out-the-sun/chinese_proverbs.

49. "Phrase Origins: It's Better to Light a Candle than to Curse the Darkness," Voices.Yahoo.com, accessed January 21, 2014, http://voices.yahoo.com/phrase-origins-its-better-light-7675652.html.

50. Corrie ten Boom, *The Hiding Place,* Goodreads.com, accessed January 21, 2014, http://www.goodreads.com/work/quotes/878114-the-hiding-place.

51. Helen Keller, "What we have once enjoyed and deeply loved we can never lose, for all that we love deeply becomes a part of us," Goodreads.com, accessed January 21, 2014, http://www.goodreads.com/quotes/search?utf8=%E2%9C%93&q=Helen+-Keller+%E2%80%93++%22What+we+have+once+enjoyed+and+deeply+loved+we+-can+never+lose%2C+for+all+that+we+love+deeply+becomes+a+part+of+us.%22++&commit=Search.

52. Quote on a headstone in Ireland, "Death leaves a heartache no one can heal, love . . .," Goodreads.com, accessed January 21, 2014, http://www.goodreads.com/quotes/17072-death-leaves-a-heartache-no-one-can-heal-love-leaves.

53. William Shakespeare, "How poor are they that have not patience! What wound did ever heal but by degrees," BrainyQuote.com, accessed January 21, 2014. http://www.brainyquote.com/quotes/quotes/w/williamsha132976.html.

54. John Wesley, Christianity.com, accessed April 29, 2014, http://www.christianity.com/11528773/.

55. Mark Twain, Goodreads.com, accessed January 21, 2014, http://www.goodreads. com/quotes/search?utf8=%E2%9C%9 3&q=Mark+Twain+%E2%80%93+Twen- ty+years+from+now+you+will+be+more+- disappointed+by+the+things+that+you+- didn%27t+do+than+by+the+ones+you+- did+do.+So+throw+off+the+bowlines.+- Sail+away+from+the+safe+harbor.+- Catch+the+trade+winds+in+your+sails.+Ex- plore.+Dream.+Discover.+&commit=Search.

56. St. Francis of Assisi, *The Little Flowers of St. Francis of Assisi*, accessed January 21, 2014, http://www.goodreads.com/author/ quotes/149151.St_Francis_of_Assisi.

57. Corrie ten Boom, "Never be afraid to trust an unknown future to . . .," Goodreads.com, accessed January 21, 2014, http://www.goodreads.com/ quotes/70125-never-be-afraid-to-trust-an-un- known-future-to-a.

58. Jean Igelow, *God's Treasury of Virtues*, (Tulsa, OK: Honor Books, 1995), 101, quoted in Elizabeth George, *A Woman's Walk with God: Growth and Study Guide* (Eugene, OR: Harvest House Publishers, 2001) 35.

59. Benjamin Malachi Franklin, "My life is but a weaving between my . . .," "The Weaver," Goodreads.com, accessed January 21, 2014, http://www.goodreads.com/quotes/489612-the- weaver-my-life-is-but-a-weaving-between-my.

60. "Book Self-Publisher FAQs for Authors and Writers," Xulon Press, the Christian Self-Publishing Company, accessed February 13, 2014, http://www.xulonpress.com/christian-self-publishing/frequently-asked-questions.php.